The Deceptive Hands of Wing Chun

by Douglas Wong

The Deceptive Hands of Wing Chun

by Douglas Wong

Copyright © 2025 I&I SPORTS SUPPLY. All rights reserved. Published by I&I SPORTS SUPPLY ISBN 978-0-934489-34-8

Dedication

To the many dedicated students of the martial arts: may this book help you to find the vital truth you are seeking. There are no secrets man cannot uncover and no techniques he cannot counter. There are no questions he cannot answer, nor teachings he cannot absorb. There is no style which is better than another.

In life, as in the martial arts, there are many pathways leading to the ultimate goal, though each may be different. May this book help you to discover this ultimate goal. May it help you to fulfill your innermost dreams.

The Path of Life

The path of life is long
The path of life has many side roads
The path of life % " s good
The path of life has evil
One can only guide you down the path i " the beginning
As you travel on there will be many opportunities available
Some good, others bad
Some right, others wrong
Some safe, others dangerous
Some rich, others poor
Wherever the path leads all will end in the same place
But how you reach it will determine your proper outlook of life
Your life is yours to live and to choose
A path to happiness
A path to peace
A path to life
Where does it lead?

Foreword

The art of Wing Chun (Beautiful Springtime) is a highly regarded fighting style. This book is the result of dedication to it.

Wing Chun is a nontraditional martial art, handed down through generations of Kung-Fu practitioners in China. It is effective, can be used in today's modern society, and is based on a straightforward, nonsense approach to achieving results—quickly.

Any knowledge, even that gained through the study of Kung-Fu, is neutral. It can, however, be used for good or bad purposes. It is the responsibility of each individual to use the knowledge presented here to honor the art of Wing Chun rather than glorify any evil which may be in their hearts.

The following pages can help you discover the wealth of knowledge within the Chinese culture. The patience, respect and discipline derived from the study of a martial art-form.

Acknowledgements

I would like to extend my deepest gratitude to Mr. Walter Wong. He helped me to understand Wing Chun's past, present and future—and more. Also, I would like to thank my senior student, Mr. Robin Kane, whom any instructor would be proud to have. Students like Robin make teaching a worthwhile venture. My sincere appreciation is also extended to Mr. Ben Makuta for his fine photographic work, and to Mr. John Davidson for his help in finalizing this task. Without their help, as well as the help of many others too numerous to mention, this book would still be nothing more than a dream.

Douglas Lim Wong

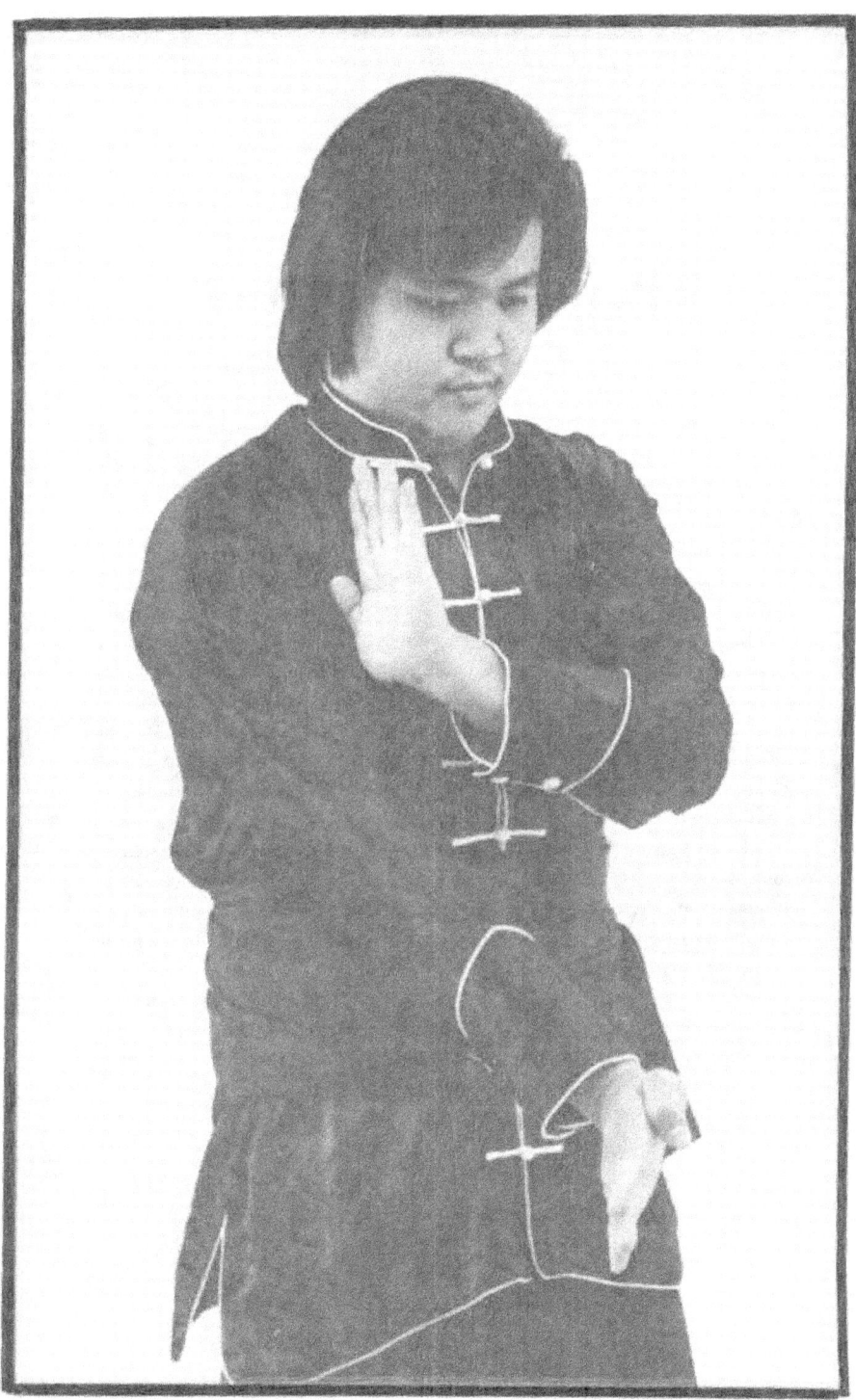

About the Author

For Sifu Douglas Lim Wong, Kung-Fu is a way of life. He has trained over two thousand students since opening his kwoon (school) in January of 1973, who have become well known for their professional demonstrations throughout the United States. His students have performed in major tournaments, movies, television shows and on lecture tours throughout the country.

Sifu Wong has studied with top instructors from a variety of Kung-Fu systems. He began as the student of Grandmaster Wong-Ark-Yuey of Los Angeles, California, who is the foremost practitioner of the Five Animals (Ng-Ying-Ga) and the Five Family (Ng-Ga-Kin) styles of Kung-Fu. Later, under Sifu Haumea "Tiny" Leflti (a senior student of Grandmaster Wong) he studied the Mok-Gar and White Crane (Bak-Hoc Pai) systems.

In 1973, under the tutelage of Master Share K. Lew, Douglas was exposed to the higher levels of Kung-Fu. Master Lew introduced him to the Taoist internal system which included herbal medicines, meditation and Taoist breathing exercises.

In 1975 Master Hsu-Hong-Chi of the God-Dragon Hsing-Yi school recommended Sifu Wong as an overseas advisor for the Taiwan-based Tang-Shou-Tao committee of the Taipei Athletics Association (the only martial arts group recognized by the Taiwan government). Sifu Wong holds the rank of 4th level in Master Hsu-Hong-Chi^ system.

Douglas has been exposed to the Yau-Kung-Men (Soft hand) style, the Bak-Fu Pai (White Tiger) style, the Bak-Mei Pai (White Eyebrow) style and the Buddhist internal system from which he drew to formulate his own system known as the White Lotus Flower style—Bai Ling Fa Pai.

Using his unique training methods, Sifu Wong has helped his students accelerate their talents beyond even their own beliefs. Since opening his kwoon in 1973 his students have amassed over five hundred trophies during a three-year span. Sifu Wong's students have consistently captured *first, second* and *third* place honors in nearly every division they have entered.

Members of Sifu Wong's Sil Lum demonstration team have appeared in the Las Vegas production of Orient 75 at the Landmark Hotel. They have been seen in television shows such as the Warner Brothers *Kung-Fu* pilot film and series, *Ironside, Police Story, Philbin/Brown & Co.*, KNBC's *Secret of the Martial Arts* (produced by Joe Vinson), CBS's *Medix, 90 Minutes,* and the Emmy nominee show *Karate, Kung-Fu and the Arts of Self-Defense* which was produced by Terry Wilson. Their movie credits include Universal Studio's *That Man Bolt* with Fred Williamson, Walt Disney's *Apple Dumpling Gang* with Bill Bixby, Don Knotts and Tim Conway, and New World Productions' *Fly Me*.

Sifu Wong was also chosen by Los Angeles mayor Tom Biadley's Blue Ribbon Committee as the Kung-Fu representative for the City of Los Angeles Martial Art Advisory Board which included such notables as Ed Parker, Bong-Soo-Han (technical advisor for the Billyjack series), Tino Tuiolesega (Grandmaster of the Lima Lama style), Steve Sanders (head of the Black Karate Federation) and Ed Hamile (chairman of the committee and a recognized leader in the Shotokan Karate movement on the West Coast).

Sifu Wong has also gained exposure through such publications as *Black Belt, Karate Illustrated, Inside Kung-Fu, Official Karate, Combat Magazine* (England), *Oriental Fighting Arts, Karate-Ka,* the *Los Angeles Free Press* and the *Los Angeles Times*. He is the author of two previous books entitled *Kung-Fu £ " e Way of Life* and *Shaolin Fighting Theories and Concepts* (Unique Publications, 1975) which are among the leading sellers on the martial arts book market today.

Contents

I.	HISTORY OF THE ART	13
II.	THE WING CHUN FAMILY TREE	18
III.	BODY ZONING AND GATES	21
IV.	BLOCKS AND STRIKES OF WING CHUN	27
V.	HAND FIGHTING AND SENSITIVITY a) Dan Chi	31
VI.	KICKS OF WING CHUN	47
VII.	CHAM KUI - SEARCHING FOR THE BRIDGE FORM #2 FORM OF WING CHUN	55
VIII.	FREE SPARRING TECHNIQUES	95
IX.	WING CHUN OTHER ASPECTS WEAPONS AND DUMMY TRAINING	105
X.	CONCLUSION	111

Chapter I

HISTORY OF THE ART

History is a subject everyone knows but few understand. Chinese historians in the past have often helped dull events become exciting stories by altering the facts. A well-trained, quickly executed technique became a magic, unblockable maneuver, or a strong, high jump into the air became an act of levitation. This, to be sure, helped to perk up the listener's ears, but made it essential for anyone interested in the facts rather than the fantasy of a well-spun yarn to separate that which happened from that which was imagined.

Myths, legends and folktales are usually tied to some kind of factual event, one way or another. Often, however, trying to realistically distinguish where the event begins and the myth leaves off is no easy task. The accurate account of Wing Chun from its historical origins to the present day is immersed in such problems which can only be straightened out after having intelligently gathered, laid out and sifted through all of the legends and facts available.

In order to present you, the reader, with more than a simple, carbon-copied story, to give you the background information which will allow you to draw your own conclusions, I have assembled three versions of the history of Wing Chun which were related to me by my instructors (and which were, in turn, related to them by their instructors).

Five people survived the burning and destruction of the original Shaolin temple—four monks and the famous nun, Ng-Mui.

Ng-Mui traveled to Fut-Shan province where she met an old friend and former disciple of the Shaolin sect, Yim San Soak, who had become a beancake vendor and manufacturer since leaving the temple.

Although Yim San Soak was highly regarded throughout the countryside, his daughter's fame wais far greater than his, for she was one of the most charming and beautiful girls in the province. Her name was Yim Wing Chun—Beautiful as Springtime.

Wing Chun's father had been training her in the traditional Shaolin style of Kung-Fu but now wanted her to begin study ing from the highly respected Ng-Mui. And, after watching the skill and determination of Wing Chun, Ng-Mui agreed to teach her a Kung-Fu system she had secretly devised. Though she had no name for the system, she considered it an extension of her previous teachings.

A rich landlord of the Fut-Shan province wanted Yim Wing Chun for his wife, though she was totally against the idea and refused to have anything to do with him.

One day the wealthy landlord came with his men and tried to take Yim Wing Chun by force. A fight broke out and her father was killed. Later, Yim Wing Chun was to avenge her father's death by killing the landlord, using her skills as a martial artist.

Yim Wing Chun continued training with Ng-Mui, eventually meeting her future husband, Chan-Fung-So, who was also skilled in the martial arts. An actor by trade, Chan was later credited with adding the weapons techniques to the system his wife had mastered. Chan named the martial style Wing Chun, after his wife.

Chan-Fung-So later tauglit his wife's system to two women, Chu- Yat-Quai and Leung-Yee-Tai. These two women passed the art to their disciple Wong-Wah-Po who in turn taught it to Leung-Jong. It was Leung Jong who taught the late, modern-day Grandmaster, Yip-Man, who brought the Wing Chun art from behind the Bamboo Curtain.

Version II

In the Ching Dynasty, Leong-Buk-Chan, a native of Canton, passed through the town of Ga San. There he met a beancake salesman destined to change his life.

Leong Buk-Chan was a young, carefree man. Ari actor by trade. He traveled from town to town giving performances of the Chinese opera.

The beancake vendor, Yim-Yee-Gung, was a popular figure in his town of Ga-San. He sold beancake to support himself and his lovely daughter. Leong Buk-Chan made such a favorable impression on the vendor when they met that he was promptly invited to the vendor's household. Leong's mannerisms and good character impressed the old gentleman, for they were qualities he admired.

In the household of Yim-Yee-Gung. Leung was introduced to the vendor's talented and lovely daughter—Yim-Wimg-Chun. The two fell in love instantly and were later married.

Yim-Yee-Gung eventually passed away, leaving his daughter to the total care of Leong-Buk-Clian. There were no family ties left for either of the two in Ga-San, so Leong took his wife tc Fu.t Shan in the province of Canton where he began teaching the martial art he had been learning from his wife—which he named Wing Chun in her honor. The name Wing Chur, had been permanently etched into martial arts antiquity when Leong Buk trained his nephew, Leong Jong, who was responsible for spreading the art throughout Canton.

Leong Jong taught his two sons, Leong-Bil and Leong-Chu, also instructing the exceptional Chan-Wah who became known as the top

Chinese Boxer in Canton. Chan-Wah was nicknamed "Jow-Chan-Wah" (money exchanger) for he was as successful a businessman as a martial artist.

Leong-Jong operated an herbal medicine shop which was located adjacent to a butcher shop. The owner of the butcher shop had a brother named Lung-Yee-Tai who was a security guard for a hotel, quite versed in the martial arts. The two shopkeepers came to know each other well and, one day, realized they both knew the same style of Kung-Fu—but from different sources.

According to Leong-Yee-Tai, when he was quite young and working on an entertainment boat, he met one of the survivors of the Shaolin monastery, Jee-Shim, who was the head of the Shaolin system. Jee-Shim came to know Leong-Yee-Tai well and decided to teach lum the style of Kung-Fu called Wing Chun which was originally the name of a temple he used as a retreat after escaping the burning of Shaolin. It was there, according to Leong-Yee-Tai, that Jee-Shim developed a version of fighting to supplement lus original Shaolin system. The Temple of the Beautiful Springtime, Wing-Chun-Tse, was the beginning of a different version of Wing Chun's history—one that is new to most martial artists, even practitioners of Wing Chun. It was Jee Shim who showed Leong-Yee-Tai the pole and butterfly-knife techniques which were later added to the Wing Chun system. The staff set was Luk Bing Bin Gwun, or the "6.5 Point Pole" techniques, in which strength and balance were essential. Leong-Yee-Tai taught these weapon forms to Leong Jong.

After Leong Jong passed away, his two sons, Leong Bil and Leong Chun, moved to Hong Kong. Their fellow classmate, Chan-Wah-Soon, stayed behind in Fut-Shan and began teaching the Wing Chun system. It was there that future Grandmaster Yip-Man received his initial Wing Chun training.

Yip-Man's father was a businessman with many enterprises throughout the country. He had businesses in Hong Kong which needed overseeing and with this in mind, Yip-Man was sent to the British Crown colony to help the business interests of his father. After a brief stay in Hong Kong, Yip-Man met Leong-Bil, the son of Leong-Jong. As he watched Yip-Man performing his Wing Chun set he learned that YipMan had studied under his classmate Chan-Wah-Soon in Fut Shan. Soon, the two became great friends and the relationship of student and instructor began yet another colorful chapter in the history of Wing Chun. Yip-Man learned the rest of the Wing Chun system from Leong Bil and became his top disciple.

When World War II broke out, Yip-Man returned to Fut Shan. He taught Wing Chun there for the duration of the war, after which he returned to Hong Kong and began teaching the art throughout the city. His first student in Hong Kong was Leong-Sheung.

Yip-Man is considered the modern-day Grandmaster of Wing Chun. He died in December 1972.

Much is owed Yip-Man for his work, contributing to the Wing Chun arts continuance and promotion throughout the world. Today, the art is taught worldwide by the Grandmasters disciples (of which the late Bruce Lee was one) and his two sons.

Version III

The Wing Chun system was founded by a woman, Yim Wing Chun, some 300 years ago. One of the most intriguing fighters in Kung-Fu's long and colorful history, Yim Wing Chun grew up in Central China where she received her initial self-defense training from a Buddhist nun of the Shaolin monastery—the famous Ng-Mui. Many nuns practiced martial arts in those days and Ng-Mui's Mui-Fa-Chuan or Plum-FlowerFist style was one of the best.

Ng-Mui was considered the top female fighter in her time. She was one of the five members who escaped the destruction of the original Shaolin temple.

The elite group were all originally Shaolin stylists but each wanted to improve on their own personal style. They completely revamped and renamed their original styles—except Monk Jee Shin Shim Shee who stuck with the traditional Shaolin system.

Ng-Mui formed the Mui-Fa-Chuan (Plum Flower Fist Style), and also the famous Mui Fa Jong (Plum Flower Fighting Stumps); Fung Doe Duk, a Taoist, created the Mok Dun San Style; Bak Mei Too Jung started the Bak Mei Pai (the White Eyebrow Style); Mew Hin Too Jung altered his style but the name was not recorded. He was also the grandfather of Fong Sai Yuk, another famous Chinese hero in the history of China.

While Yim Wing Chun was learning the Mui-Fa-Chuan from Ng-Mui, she saw that the system was too complicated and placed too much emphasis on power techniques and strong horse stances. Knowing that she could not develop enough power to match a larger, more powerful adversary, she wanted to develop a style that would best suit her body. She was looking for the simplest, least complicated, most efficient means of defending herself. After years of searching, she decided to create her own. The resulting art is known today as Wing Chun or Beautiful Springtime. It is a brutally effective combat system which stresses economical movement and angular attacks.

Yim Wing Chun's system was an entirely new, close-quarter method of combat. Twice as fast as any other system, its main features were economy of movement, directness of action, a unique type of straight punch, and the famous sticking hands practice known as "Chi Sau."

Yim Wing Chun taught the art to her husband, an actor, already well versed in the martial arts. He is credited with incorporating the traditional Chinese weapons into the system. Even today the serious student of Wing Chun still undergoes training in the use of the traditional weapons, though the stance for the weapon training is lower and much wider than the basic boxing stance. This is due to the weight and balance of each of the traditional weapons.

Based on the theory that the shortest distance between two points is a straight line, Wing Chun lacks the elongated, flowing motions which are part of most other forms of Kung-Fu. The Wing Chun practitioner draws an imaginary line, running down the center of the body. He uses this pivotal line as the main axis around which blocks and strikes revolve. When in combat, Wing Chun practitioners are taught to have their centerline directly opposite the opponents chin.

In many Gung-Fu systems, there are up to one hundred hand forms, or kuens. The forms are prearranged patterns of movement which imitate the concept of fighting opponents in given direction. Here, the Wing Chun system differs considerably from other styles as there are only three forms. They are Sil-Lum-Tao, or "The Small Idea Form"; Cham-Kui, or "Searching for the Bridge Form"; and BiMee or "Flying Fingers Form."

The Wing Chun stylist starts training in the first set, Sil-Lum-Tao, which is the building block of Wing Chun. It shows the basic blocks and parries necessary to offset an adversary. Then he progresses through Cham-Kui and Bil-Jee. Between the beginning stage and the advance stage a student is introduced to Chi-Sao, or the famous [44]"Sticking Hand" practice. This exercise is based on sensitivity, reflexes, coordination and timing. In the advanced stages the exercise is done blindfolded, teaching one to overcome an opponent. A good Wing Chun man can tie your hands up and neutralize your attacks before they get started.

Training in Luk-Sau, or double hand sparring, and Lap-Sao, ward-off hands techniques, are taught in conjunction with fighting. After learning most of the techniques, a Wing Chun stylist is ready for the Mook-Yan-Jong, or "Wooden Man Dummy," which utilizes over one hundred different movements of the hands and feet. The training simulates every conceivable situation. It is the culmination of Wing Chun training, along with blindfold fighting.

Invented by a woman, Wing Chun is probably one of the better styles for the woman seeking to learn self-defense. The style complements an opponents strength. It is an aggressive style, with compact, economical attacks and defenses. But again, no style is any better than the effort put forth to master it.

Chapter II

THE WING CHUN FAMILY TREE

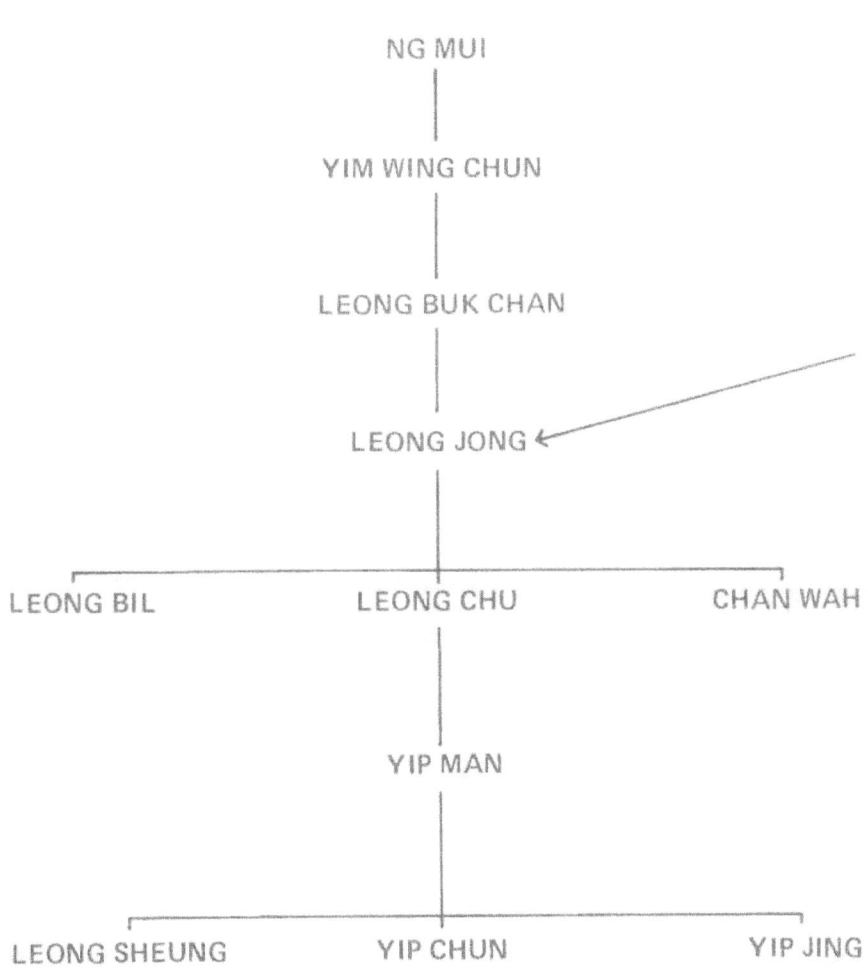

JEE SHIM

LEONG YEE TAI

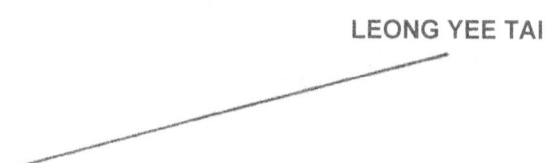

1) . NG MUI - " *famous Shaolin Nun who taught Yim Wing Chun her secret system.*
2) . YIM WING CHUN — *credited as the founder of the Wing Chun system.*
3) . LEONG BUK CHAN — *the husband of Yim Wing Chun. He taught his nephew the Wing Chun system.*
4) . LEONG JONG — *the nephew of Leong Buk Chan. He was responsible for spreading the Wing Chun Art all over Canton.*
5) . LEONG BIL — *son of Leong Jong, taught Yip Man the final stages of Wing Chun.* LEONG CHU — *the second son of Leong Jong.*
6) . CHAN WAH — *nickname Jow Chan Wah(meaning Money exchanger),* was considered the top boxer in Canton China. He was Yip Man's first instate tor,
7) . YIP MAN — *Grandmaster of Wing Chun in the Modern era spreading the Wing Chun system all over Hong Kong. (He taught the late famous Bruce Lee).*
8) . LEONG SHEUNG — *was the first student of Yip Man.*
9) . YIP CHUN / YIP JING — *the sons of Yip Man.*
10) . JEE SHIM — *considered the father of* the *Shaolin system after the burning of the Shaolin Temple. He taught Leong Yee Tai his Wing Chun system.*
11) . LEONG YEE TAI — *learn " ze weaponry and Wing Chun system a " d taught Hie weapons to Leong Jong.*

Chapter III

BODY ZONING AND GATES

The human body is the source of awesome power capable of creating or destroying its surrounding environment. That which controls this power is the human mind, for it determines the good or evil involved in each endeavor. The mind alerts and unites the body into a single fighting unit which can deal with the problem at hand.

Different blows to the body can render a person helpless; one must be well versed in protecting his own main striking area, and know how to attack his opponent's vulnerable points. Body zoning is an art in itself. The body is divided and protected in a logical sequence of maneuvers.

The top half of the body is protected by the upper extremities: the hand, wrist, forearm, elbow and shoulder. Each area can be used to deflect or to block attempted attacks. In defense, the hands are the quickest for most people. They are flexible and capable of changing direction in midair. The legs are less controllable. There are numerous conditioning exercises for the hands used by Wing Chun stylists. The Chi-Sao (double sticking-hand), Luk Sao (Warding-Off Hand), Dahn-Chi 㟻ingle Sticking-Hand), Muk Yan Jong (Wooden Man Dummy), and sandbag punching are all methods for conditioning the hands. Soft practice develops sensitivity while hard, external practice conditions the entire arm to take punishment—as well as give it.

The top half of the body is divided into four zones. There are specific blocking techniques for each zone or area being attacked. But, of course, a person must learn to fight according to the prevailing situation. There are no unchangeable patterns to follow when a person encounters an adversary. The rule is to accomplish what is necessary in the shortest time possible. The following are a few rules to follow when fighting.

1. Learn to block with the minimum amount of distance to deflect an oncoming attack. Never over-block the opponent's attack and leave yourself open.
2. When practicing free-fighting, vary the speed in order to understand your blocking zone.

3. Use your legs and hips in conjunction with the upper half of your torso. This will increase your power and striking distance.
4. Do not back off once you have your opponent on the run. Keep the pressure on throughout the fight and adjust your zones as you change to different fighting techniques and angles.

The entire body can be divided into three levels: (1) the upper-gate: from the chest region to the top of the head; (2) the middle-gate: from the heart region to the groin; and (3) the lower-gate, which consists of the entire leg region from hip, down to the toes.

Most Wing Chun kicks are kept in the lower-gate region and go no higher than the groin area, but there are exceptions. A practitioner should never go beyond the chest region in any real fighting encounter. The hands are capable of protecting the upper and middle-gate regions while the legs are used in sliding motions, or low checking kicks to avoid a leg attack from reaching one's body.

Study the following pictures and diagrams and try to understand some of the principles involved in the zoning process.

FRONT VIEW: The body is subdivided into three horizontal levels or gates. The gates are (1) high gate, which consists of the chest region to the top of the head; (2) the middle gate, which contains the heart region down to the groin area; (3) and the lower gate, which consists of the entire leg region from the hips to the toe region. The body is also subdivided into right and left half by a vertical line drawn through the middle of the body.

SIDE VIEW: The body is divided into four zones which consist of the front half and the rear half, that is also divided into a high and middle gate zoning.

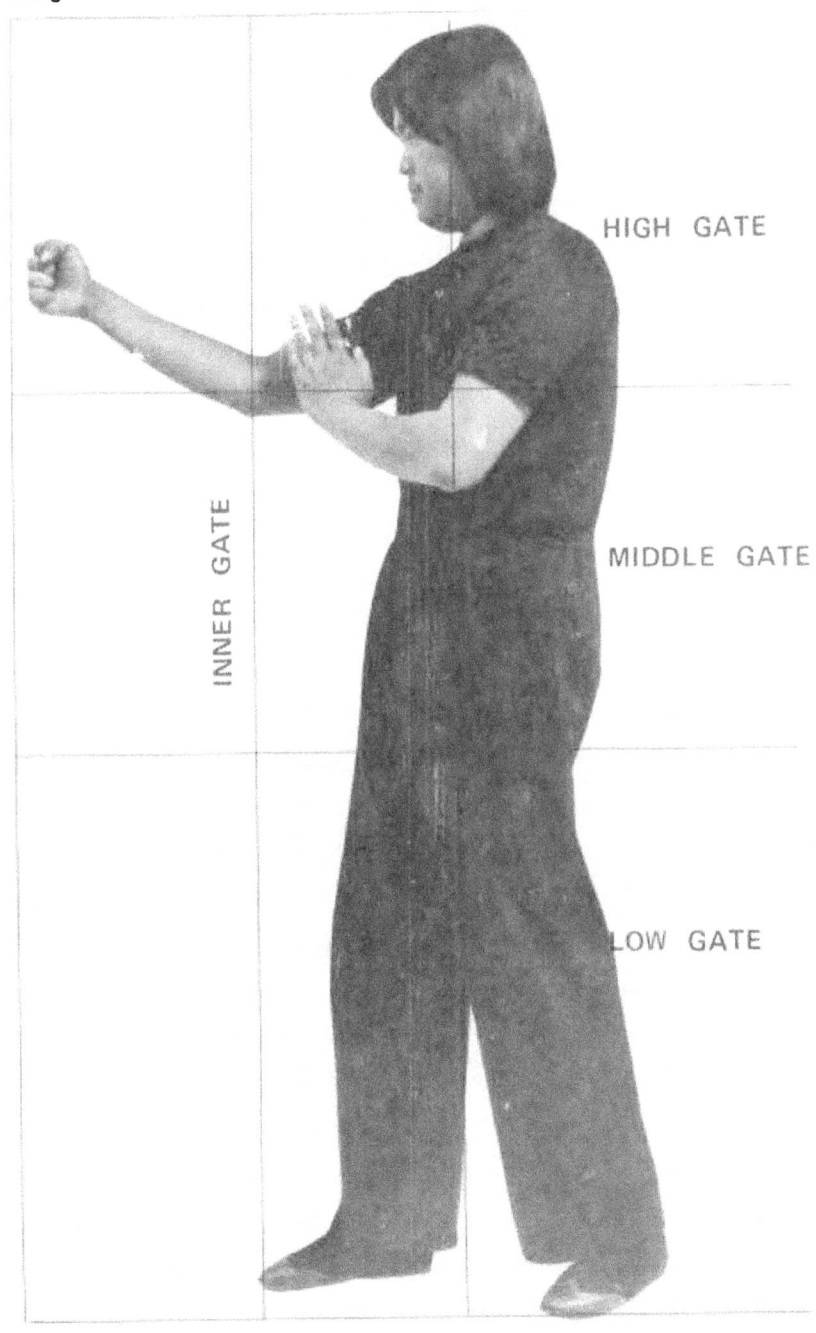

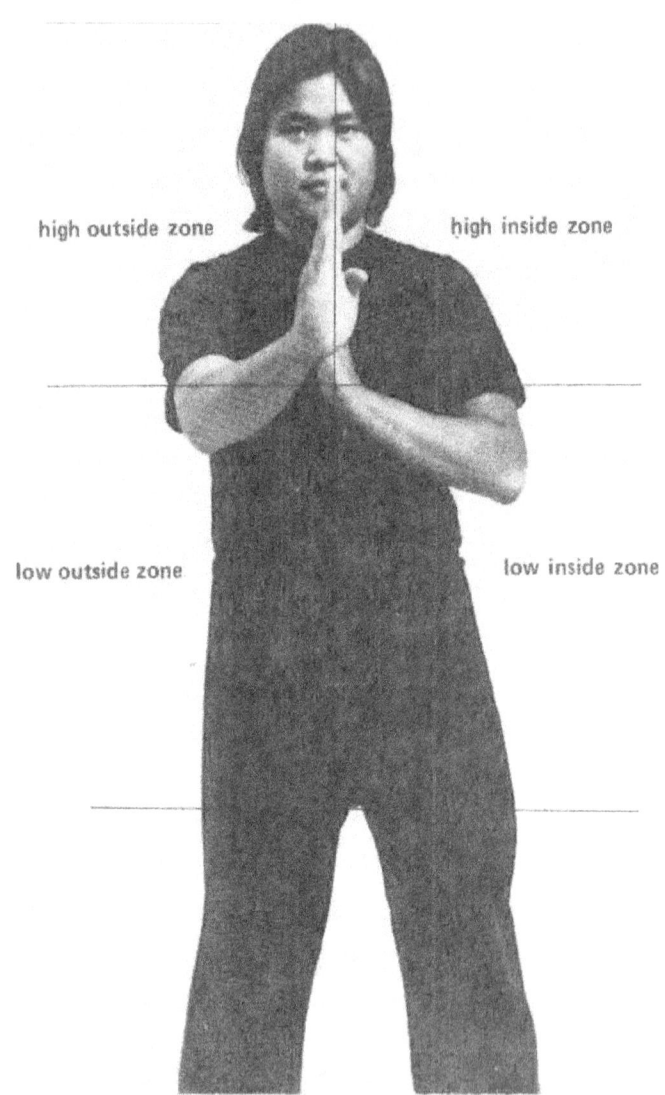

FRONT VIEW OF THE UPPER BODY: The top half of the body can be divided into four zones namely: (1) high inside zone; (2) high outside zone; (3) low inside zone; (4) and the low outside zone. There are specified blocks used for each allotted area in order to maximize the effort of the minimal power used.

Chapter IV

BLOCKS AND STRIKES OF WING CHUN

There are very few blocks and strikes used in the Wing Chun system which could be called "flowery." The main purpose of Wing Chun is to get the most done with the least effort necessary. The blocks of Wing Chun are actually *deflections*, not direct-power blocks; they are used in conjunction with body-twisting and punching-angle. A slight twist of the hips can turn a weak block to one that is strong and centralized as long as the centerline theory is followed. The Wing Chun stylist is taught that a deflection is just as powerful or effective as a punch. A good block can set an opponent up for an attack, but remember that the block never goes past the center blocking region (study the chapter on Body Zoning).

The strikes in Wing Chun are simple. They consist of the regular vertical punch, the uppercut, and the finger jabs. The forms help to develop the power necessary to learn correct blocking and punching in Wing Chun. The power of the punches is generated from the waist. The arms transfer this power in pulley-like fashion to the fists. The Allowing are some of the basic movements used in the Wing Chun system.

FRONT VIEW: Basic Wing Chun "Straight Punch" or jik chung. The punch is used along the centerline of the body with the elbow kept in close to the body. The tucked-in position increases the power of one's punches and also provides added speed while cutting down the distance of your target.

SIDE VIEW: The bottom three knuckles are used in a rising motion; always keep the elbow close to the body to maximize the exposed area.

SIDE VIEW: Finger Jab. The finger jab is one of the most useful hand strikes used in Wing Chun. In the third set, "Bil Jee" (Flying Fingers or Shooting Fingers), this technique is very evident. The finger jab can be used to strike an opponent in the eye region and is especially good to use when a person leans away from your punches. The open fingers give you the extra inches that may determine the outcome of your fight.

FRONT VIEW: Keep all the fingers together and thrust forward keeping the thumb in to reinforce the finger jab.

DOWN BLOCK: The bottom hand is used as a defensive measure against low attacks. The opposite hand is always kept up higher to defend the upper portion of the body.

Reverse side of the previous exercise.

DOUBLE BLOCK: The upper hand is used as a high outside block while the bottom hand is used as a low outside block. The hand can be converted into an attack at any given time and not just for blocking.

Other side of Double Block.

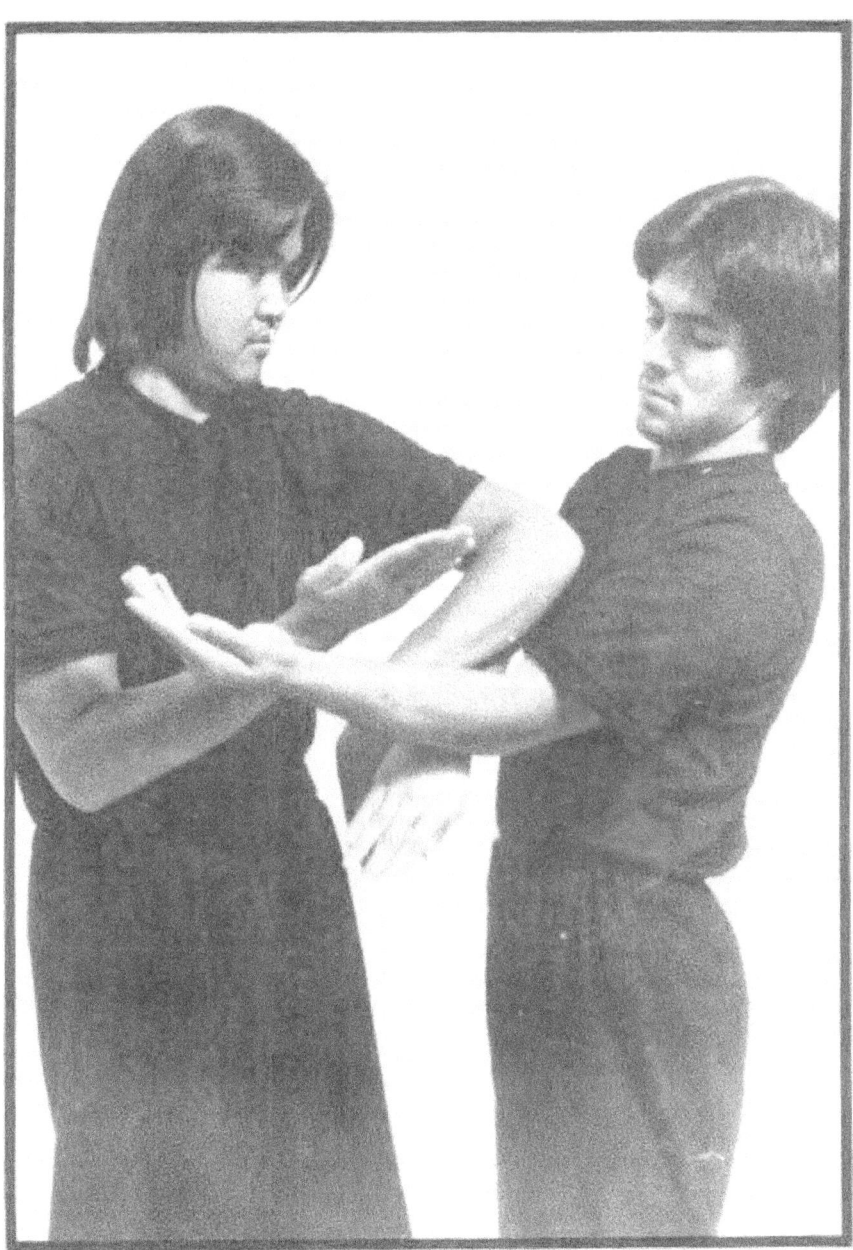

Chapter V

HAND FIGHTING AND SENSITIVITY

In the Wing Chun system some of the most deceptive techniques are concealed in the hand-fighting methods. The famous "Chi-SaeJ or "Sticking Hand Fighting" is the trademark of this highly sophisticated system. The exercises are not meant for fighting, but for the development of sensitivity throughout the entire arm region, from fingertips to the shoulders. Arm contact creates awareness of the strength applied by an opponent, and the direction his arms move while searching for an opening.

The Chi-Sao exercises are complex but simple. To begin this training, a person Hrst completes form one (Sil-Lum-Tao). The Sil-Lum-Tao teaches basic movements including the basic punch, the stationary front-horse, elbow-tucked-in techniques, circling wrist, upward-hand block and the finger jabs. After the first set is completed the students are introduced to the more advance horses to be used in the second and third sets (Cham Kui and Bil Jee). Here, 2 more advance blocking methods are introduced. All this leads to the more advance sticking hand training methods. Kicking is taught to develop balance and to add the additional techniques necessary to complete the Wing Chun arsenal.

The basic hand exercise is Dahn-Clii, *Single-Hand Fighting*, which incorporates the six fundamental hand techniques found in Sil-Lum- Tao. The six techniques are (1) fook-sao (elbow-in block); (2) tahn-sao (the palm-up block); (3) Yun-jeong (the vertical palm heel strike); (4) Depressing palm heel; (5) Bong-Sao {the elbow-in the air block); and (6) the vertical punch or jik-chung.

The movement of Dahn-Chi are performed in the front-horse stance, close enough to your partner so you need not lean into him when launching your attack.

The idea of this exercise is not to overpower your opponent by using brute strength but by applying just enough pressure to feel the direction of the oncoming attack. Use enough strength to deflect your opponent's attack and counter quickly when the opening is felt.

This exercise uses one side, then the other to develop the hands. The hands must become one coordinated unit in order to derive the proper benefits of the double sticking-hand.

The phase of exercise which follows single-hand fighting is the double-sticking-hand. This unique exercise develops sensitivity and timing to razor sharpness. The sticky hand has many different patterns to follow. Here we will discuss some of the basic patterns.

1. The first pattern consists of placing one hand on the inside and one on the outside of the opponent's hands.

2. The second pattern is performed with both hands placed on the inside of the opponent's hands.

3. The third pattern is performed with both hands placed on the outside of the opponets hands.

Only after the student becomes adept at perceiving punches and kicks by sight is he ready to move on to the sensitivity training of Wing Chun in which he learns to perceive through the sense of touch.

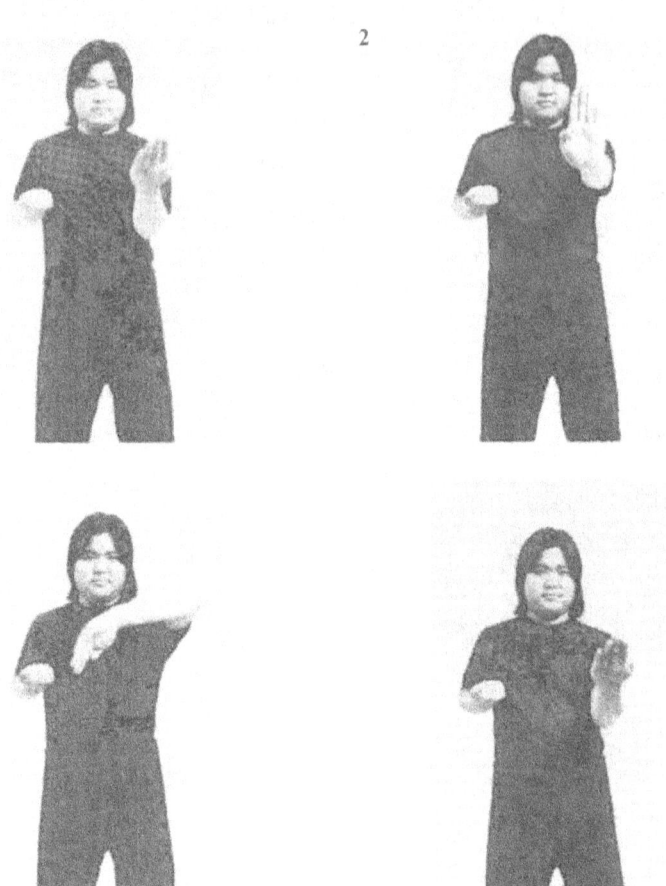

1. The practitioner assumes a front horse stance with the right arm pulled back to the side. The left arm is held in front of the body with the palm facing up (tan sao or palm-up block).

2. The hand is extended with a palm strike to the opponent's body.

3. Raise the elbow up while the hand is angled downward as if you were looking at your watch.

4. Return to the original position with the palm-up block. Your training partner would perform the following movement as you perform the previous movement. Make sure that you remain in the front horse and use the opposite hand to work with each other.

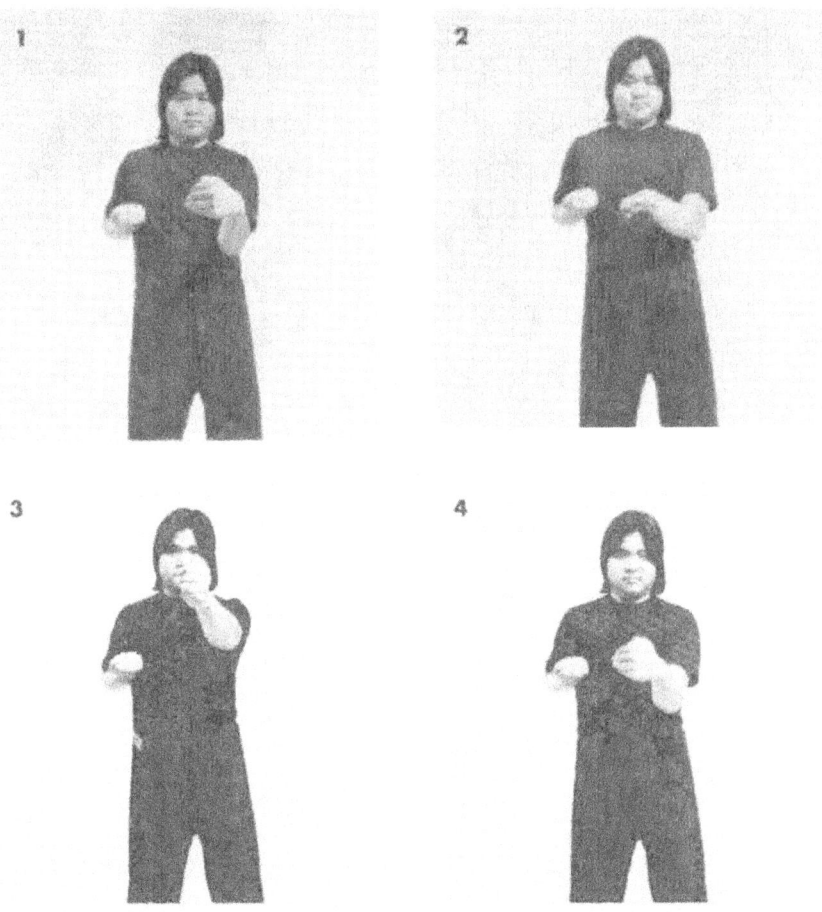

1. Assume front horse position with one arm pulled back to the side while the opposite arm is in front with a elbow bent in blocking position.

2. Pull the hand in toward your body using a depressing palm block which redirects the opponent's hand from reaching his target.

3. Convert the blocking hand into an offensive punching attack which is aimed toward your opponents facial area.

4. Drop your hand back into an elbow bent in position with the wrist turned inward and down.

The following is the combination of the two previous exercises.

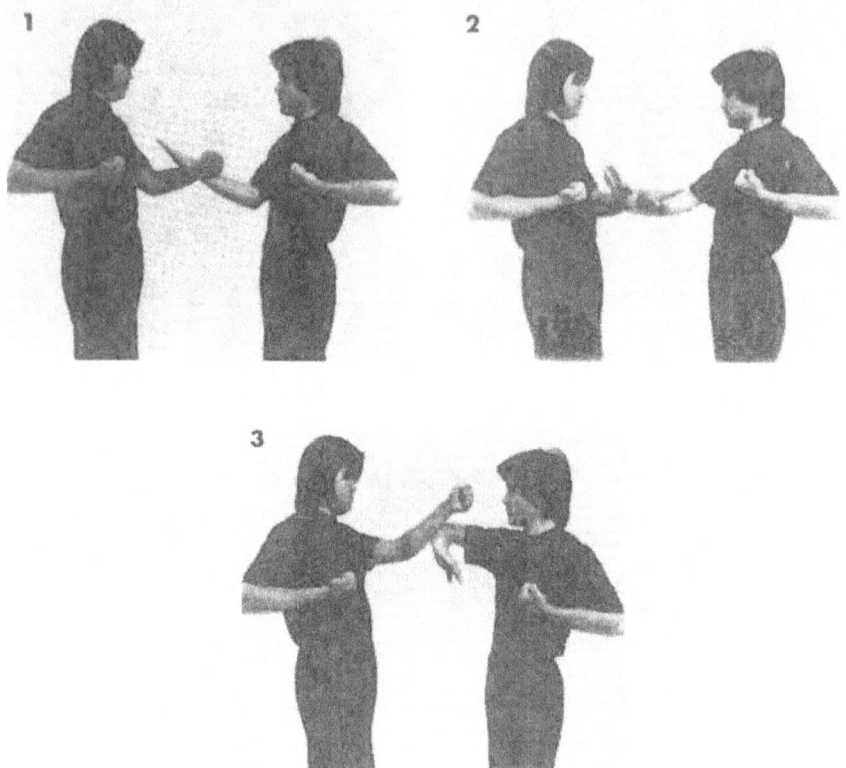

1. Ready position. The practitioner on the right is in a palm-up blocking position while the opponent on the left is in an elbow tucked-in position with the wrist on top of his partner.

2. The practitioner on the right delivers a palm strike which is met with a depressing palm block.

3. The practitioner on the left converts his block hand into a punch toward the head region which is blocked by your partner with a rising elbow block (bong sao).

Bring both hands down to original position and repeat the exercise until you are tired then change to other hand to complete both sides.
*This exercise is not actual fighting but an art on developing the sensitivity in your upper extremities. The motions are done smoothly and contact is your most important requirement. Without the hand in constant contact your opponent can easily feel an opening and render you helpless.

Double Sticking Hands—Seong Chi
There are many patterns for double sticking hand. Here we will demonstrate a few of the different variations such as double inner hand, double outer hands, inside-outside hand, all of these are different hand positioning each having its advantages and its weaknesses.

The right arm is positioned up in the air (bong sao) while the left hand is in an elbow tucked in hooking position (fook sao).

Rotate the hand clockwise into a right palm-up block (tan sao) and a left inside wrist hook.

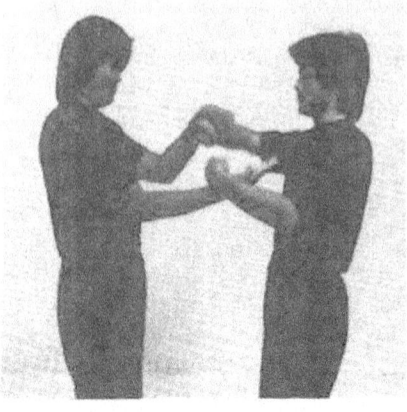 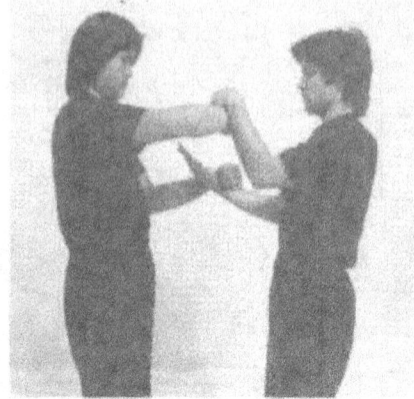

Combining the movements with a partner. This exercise has both practitioners doing the same movement but in different sequences. Keep the hands going at a regular pace and later speed up the process. This particular Chi Sao deals with one hand on the inside while one hand works outside of your opponent's hand defense.

Keep the hand in contact and try to feel your opponent's movement. This is very important to start making your arm very sensitive to slight pressure because when you reach the advance stage of blindfold fighting it will definitely come in handy.

Double Inner Hands Pattern. Your right hand is in a palm-up defense while the left hand is in an elbow-up blocking position.

Rotate the arm until the opposite hand replaces the other while reversing the hand-blocking technique.

The man on the right will be using double outer hand while the person on the left will be using double inner hand. The man on the right has his right hand in a high wrist hook on top of opponent's raising elbow block, his left hand is in an elbow-tucked position while his opponent has a palm up block.

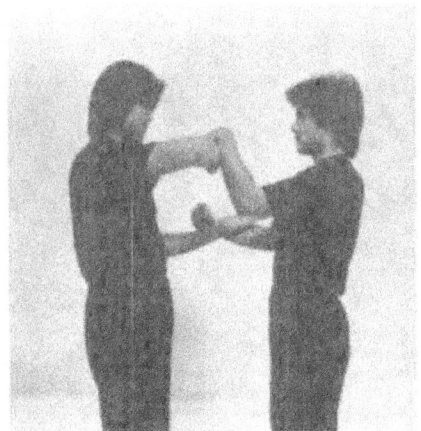

Now rotate the two hands while your opponent follows your motion. The hands merely switch to the opposite hand defense while following the back and forth motion. Continue the motion till one gets tired and then switch position of the hands. After one gets proficient in this exercise then the techniques can be applied which will be shown in the upcoming series.

The Double Outer Hand Position. The right arm is in an elbow-tucked- in position while the left hand is in a high wrist block.

Rotate the hand and switch the hand positioning.

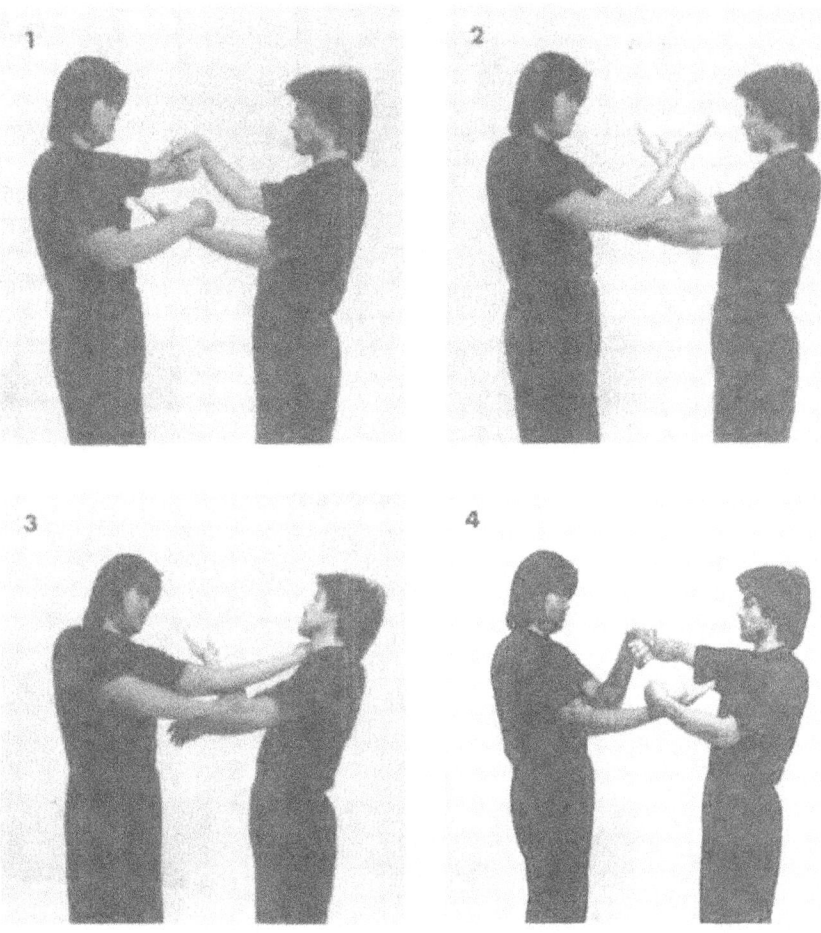

1. Ready position with the hand in place for the inside and outside sequences.
2. Sifu Wong uses an outside block which forces Si-Hing Kane's hand to the outside, while his right hand is being used in a depressing palm block.
3. Sifu Wong then shifts his body into a side leaning horse and strikes out with an open hand blow to the jugular vein while the left hand still maintains control of the opponent's hand.
4. Sifu Wong switches hand position this time.

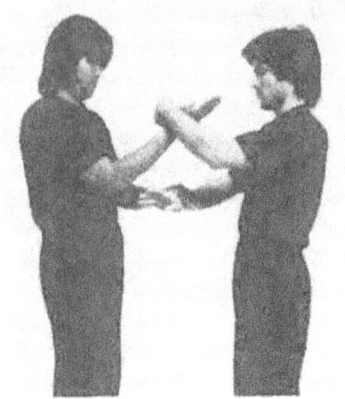
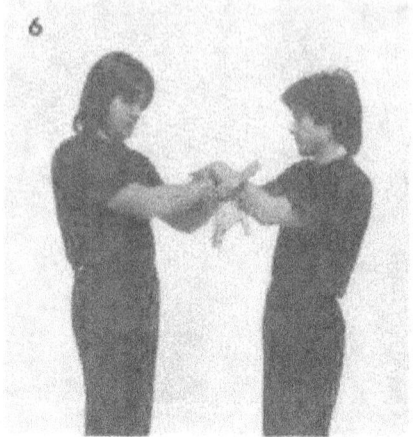

5   Sifu Wong drops his left arm downward while using his right arm to raise the opponents arm upward.

6   Sifu Wong uses his left arm pressing the opponents right hand into his left hand, thus forming a crossing block (making sure your hand circles underneath with the fingers ready to cross grab).

7   Slide your right arm from in between his hands and slide it into the opponents neck region while the opposite hand maintains control of his hands.

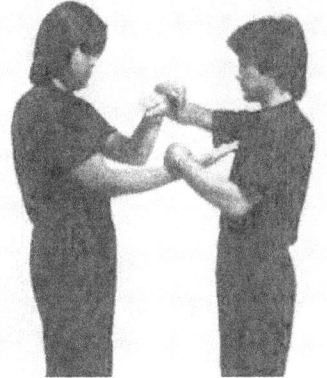 

1. Ready position.

2. Rotate the arm to position number two of the exercise.

3. As the arm rotates back to position #1 shift your horse from a front horse into a side leaning horse which forces your opponent to the outside and press in with your left hand punching to the ribs.

4. Shift your body and horse to the opposite side and convert the blocking hand into an open hand strike to the neck region. Using your left hand in a pressing palm block to maintain control of your opponent.

5. Pull your body back to opposite side and use the striking hand in a neck grab, then turn your left blocking hand into a punch to the face. The constant shifting keeps your opponent off balance and doubles your punching power.

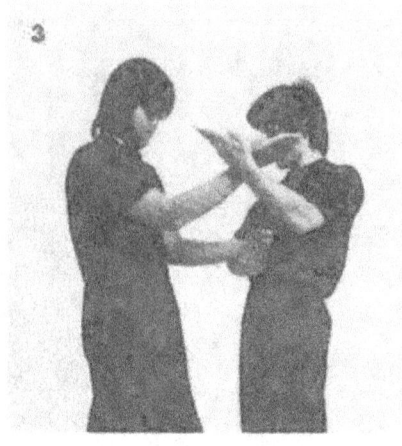

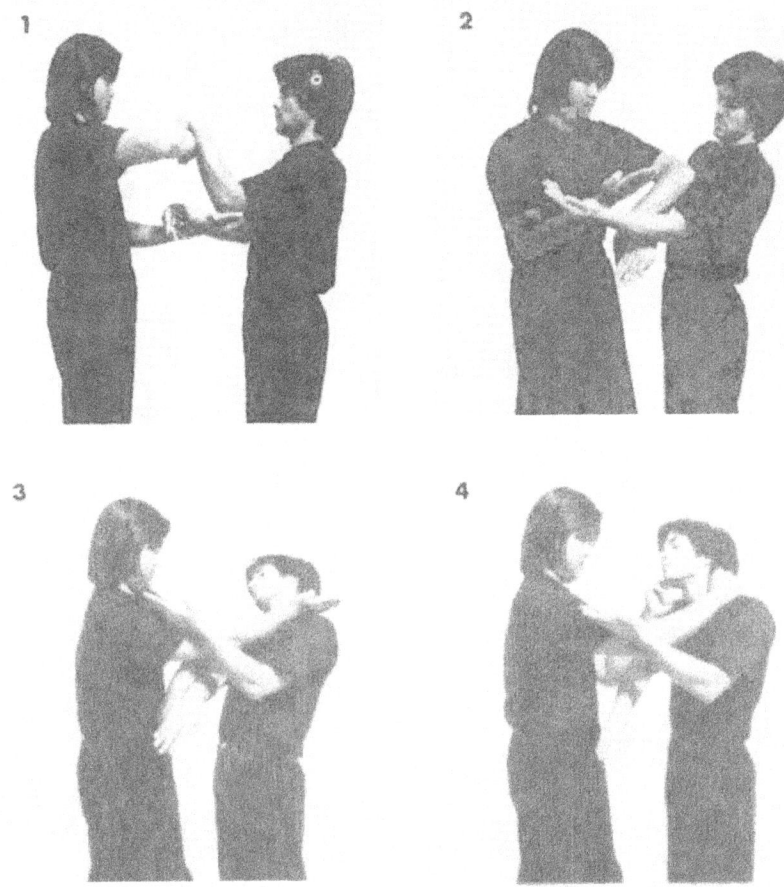

1. Assume starting position with the opponent on the right in a double outer position while opponent on the left in a double inner position.

2. Rotate the hand to position #2 of exercise but the opponent on the left continues the motion and overrides the opponent's defense by using an elbow strike to the chest. This movement was created by using the opposite hand to open up the defense of your opponent and also shift your body in to close the gap between the bodies.

3. Shifting back to the other side maintain control of opponent's right hand and use your own right hand to strike the neck region.

4. Grab the back of the neck before the opponent can set up his offense and apply a rising punch to opponent's jaw to finish him off.

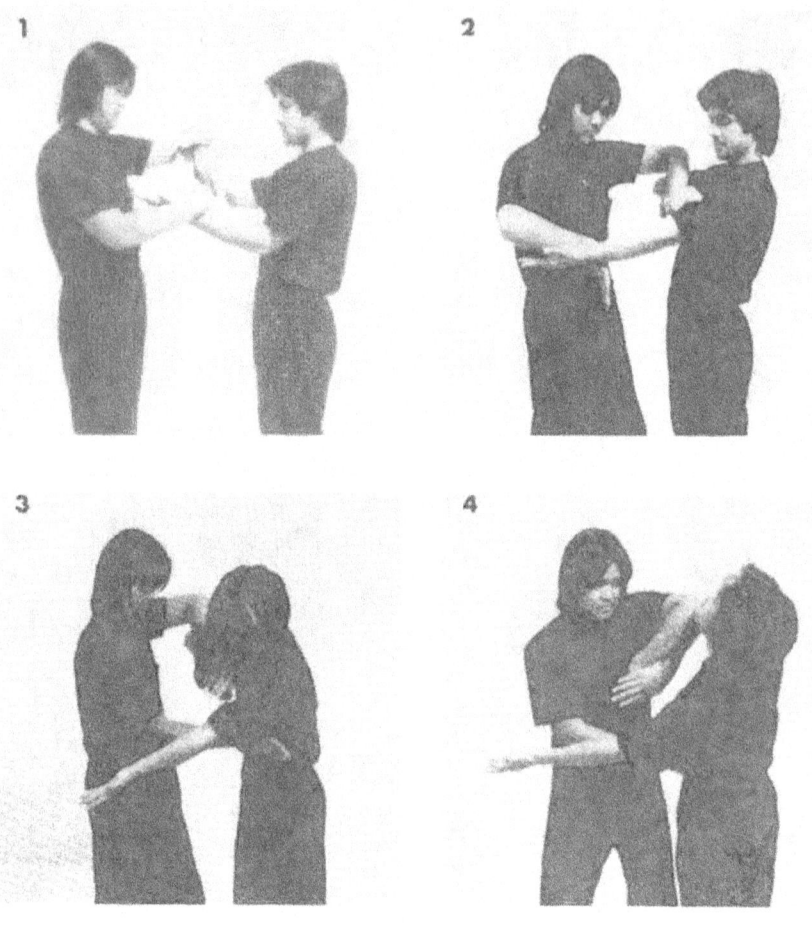

1 Ready position.

2 Opponent on the left uses a right circling block which pushes the opponent's hand to the outside, the left hand is used in a hooking motion and presses inward while the elbow is raised to apply leverage to the body.

3 Shift the body toward the left side and apply a palm strike to the rib area which forces the victim toward his right side.

4 Before opponent can evade the palm strike use the opposite side and apply an elbow strike to the face area and shift your body to double your power.

Chapter VI

KICKS OF WING CHUN

Wing Chun kicks are direct and effective. They are used in attacking weak points of the lower torso: the knees, shins, ankles, insteps, calf muscles and groin region.

Kicks are limited in Wing Chun to the most practical for use in actual combat. Wing Chun stylists are taught to use their kicks to counter other kicks whenever possible (blocking a kick with a kick). They must learn to move in on an opponent who is kicking and never to step away or run back. The natural reaction of man is to move back when a kick is launched against him but this only puts him into his opponents kicking zone. Try to maintain constant pressure on an opponent so he cannot maintain the balance to throw a kick and never allow a kick to reach its power zone (the last stage of the kick). Try to jam, block or deflect a kick before it gets started.

In Wing Chun the practitioner is taught to keep his kicks below the waist. A high kick disrupts your balance and exposes your body to danger. In reality, high kicks are appealing for flashy, showy movements and are good for obtaining flexibility as an exercise-not for fighting.

The thrusting power of the kicks is obtained by using the whole body in a forward sliding motion. The momentum gained by the sliding motion in conjunction with the effective striking surface (the heel) can upset an opponents defense and render a quick and decisive victory. The entire leg-region is connected to the heel—making this the most powerful striking implement in the kicking arsenal.

The combination of using your calf and thigh muscles properly shoots your foot out in a piston like stroke. The toes are pulled back to make the heel stronger and allow greater concentration on this particular area. Correct thrusting, angling and power can easily disable your opponent with a broken limb or serious injury. The following are rules to remember for the kicking techniques of Wing Chun:

1. Never throw a high kick unless it is certain it will finish your opponent. Your hands are quicker and can handle the same type of attack with a greater margin of safety.

2. Keep your kicks low, detracting your opponent's attention, and allow your hands to work.

3. Do not broadcast your kicks.

4. Try to control your opponent's kicking range. Maintain your own proper range. Move in and out quickly.

1 Front horse position with the hand guarding the center line.

2 Draw your right leg up with the knee raised and the toes pulled up.

3 Extend the leg outward in front of your body with a front heel thrust kick while maintaining the hand positioning.

By using the same first two movements you then shift the body sideways to launch a side heel kick. The heel is your most pcwerfuil striking surface; make sure you take full advantage of its power. Always pull your toes back toward you to keep them from getting hurt and to concentrate all the focus power into the heel region.

The cross heel kick which is used in kicking to the opponent's shin or knee area. The cross kick is one of the most useful kicks which can stun an opponent for a split second which is enough time for you to finish him off with a hand attack.

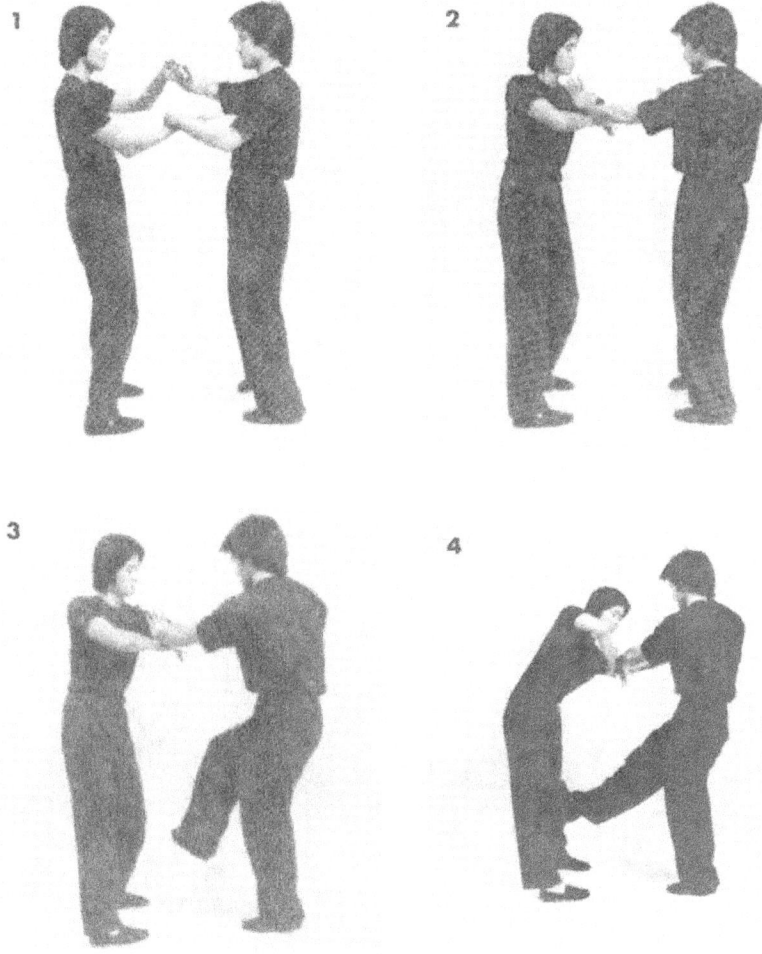

1. Assume basic ready position.
2. Opponent on the right shifts his weight to the right and applies an inward palm strike which pushes the opponent off balance.
3. The opponent on the right raises his right leg and aims toward the knee area.
4. The opponent on the right then pulls the opponent's arms and apply a cross heel kick to the knee area which can damage the leg permanently.

1 Ready position.
2 Opponent on the left attempts a right cross kick.
3 Before the kick can reach its destination Si-Hing Kane applies a right scooping kick that deflects the opponents kick which causes him to lose his balance slightly.
4 Quickly shifting his weight. Si Hing Kane then applies a right side heel kick to the opponents standing leg.

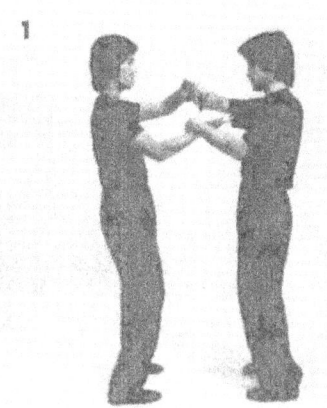

1 Ready position.

2 Si-Hing Kane shifts into a left side horse while pushing his opponent's Si-Hing Kodani's arm into the opposite direction.

3 Then Si Hing Kane continues the motion and presses the opponent off balance by pushing into the elbow region, then sending a front heel kick to the groin.

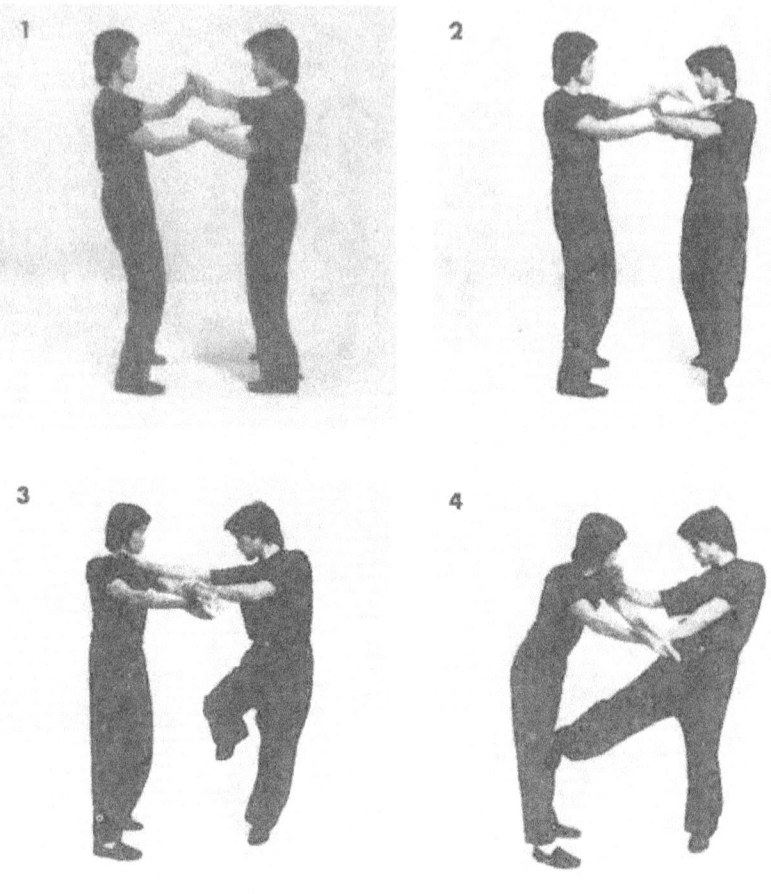

1 Ready position.
2 Shift the body into a right leaning horse while using your left hand to hook the opponent's opposite arm.
3 Using a cross grab and pulling the opponents arm into each other, apply a strike to the neck while drawing your leg up.
4 Release a side kick into your opponent's knee and continue the pressure with your arms. A follow-up technique with punches will finish off your opponent.

Chapter VII

CHAM KUI -
SEARCHING FOR THE BRIDGE FORM
#2 FORM OF WING CHUN

Wing Chun forms look simple. To the untrained eye the form seems little more than simple punches and kicks. This often leaves observers wondering just how such movements could possibly be used in self defense, for most occidentals are used to the brawls of western movies. Neither the movie brawls of Hollywood, nor the Kung-Fu and Karate fights now in vogue, are true accounts of actual combat. They are make-believe fight scenes set up by stuntmen and producers to create excitement for the untrained public.

Forms are used in Wing Chun to develop a source of exercises to be utilized by either hand. The very short, tight movements are used to simulate fighting tactics which can be used in any given situation. The forms develop the power and focus necessary to control the direction of one's body movement.

Cham-Kui, Searching the Bridge, is the second form in the Wing Chun system which has more advanced movements compared to the first set, Sil-Lum-Tao. Without Sil-Lum-Tao, however, and its basic movements, the second form does not have the solid foundation upon which to build the more advanced techniques. The first set is involved with coordinating the hands and eyes to develop the strength necessary for proper striking and blocking. The second set is used to develop body shifting and kicking. Set one was stationary, but the Cham-Kui set teaches mobility, using the sliding motion of the legs.

If you have seen Cham-Kui before, you may notice a few more kicks in this version of the form. This is due to the fact that different disciples of Yip-Man stress the importance of leg maneuvers as well as those of the hands. In the development of the legs in fighting it is important to maintain balance and steady pressure on one's opponent while driving into him. Master the simple, direct kicks of the Wing Chun and you will have added considerably to your fighting arsenal.

The first form, Sil-Lum-Tao, took Yip-Man almost an hour to complete. His strength and focus was close to perfect. Today, many students of various styles are in a rush to get through a form, and tend to forget the basic foundation. The form must be practiced every day with strength and power, focusing control on the muscles involved with each movement. The kuen (form) strengthens the body both internally and externally sharpening the reflexes. It develops agility and teaches balance as well as the ability to handle any situation.

Cham-Kui is the intermediate form spanning Sil-Lum-Tao and Bil-Jee (Flying Finger Form), and connects the knowledge of the two sets. A book in the near future will cover the aspects of the third set, which is far more complicated to perform. Try to maintain a steady pace while performing this set (Cham-Kui) and apply dynamic tension principles to each and every muscle utilized in the movements.

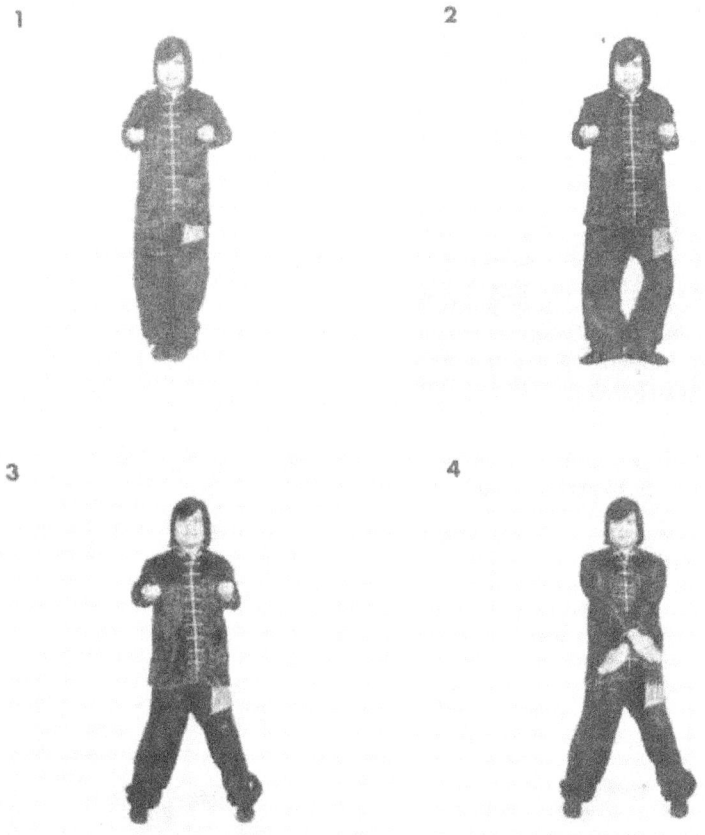

1 Starting position with feet together and arm drawn up under your armpit area.
2 Spread the toe outwardly to 45-degree angle.
3 Slide your heel out till your feet are pointing straight, sinking the weight down with the knee bent in slightly.
4 Shoot both hands downward into a cross hand position with the right hand on top.
5 Turn the hand upward toward your chest with the palms coming in toward your chest with the arm crossed.
6 Withdraw the hands to the side of your body.

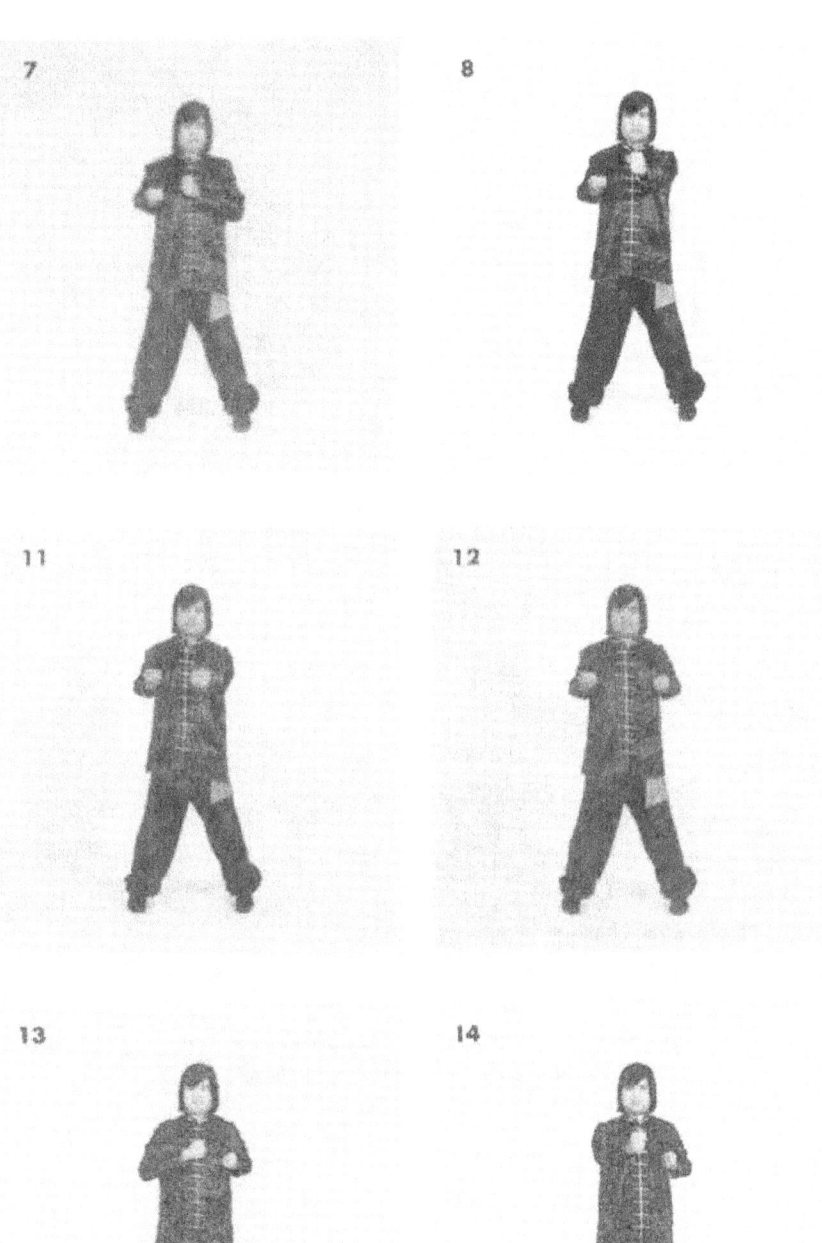

9   10

    left fist along the chest until it is positioned in the center of t.

    le fist outwardly keeping the elbow tucked in and slightly bent along the centerline.

9 Open the hands while turning the fingers upwardly. Keep the hand in the center.

1 0 Twist the wrist with the fingers pointing downward.

1 1 Withdraw the hand back to your side.

2 2 Close your hand in a grabbing motion with the palm still facing down.

3 3 Using the right hand run the fist along the side of your chest region until it is in the centerline position.

1 4 Extend the fist out away from your body along the centerline.

59

15   16

19   20

21   22

15 Turn the hand down counterclockwise till the fingers are pointed down.

16 Open the hand up as you rotate the fingers to palm-upward position.

17 Close the hand in a grabbing motion with the palm still down.

18 Withdraw the hand until it reaches the original spot underneath the armpit area.

19 Extend both hands outwardly and twist both hands with the two palms facing each other.

20 Withdraw the hand and pull the right arm on top of the left arm with the fingers still extended with palm downward.

21 Now the form will start shifting into different horses and body movement which separate it from the first set, Sil Lum Tao, which was a stationary set. First turn the body toward the left side while keeping the arms in the same position when shifting.

22 Switch to the right side making sure the toe of the front leg is pointed to the front with the back leg bent and to the side. Keep most of the weight on the rear leg.

23 24

27 28

29 30

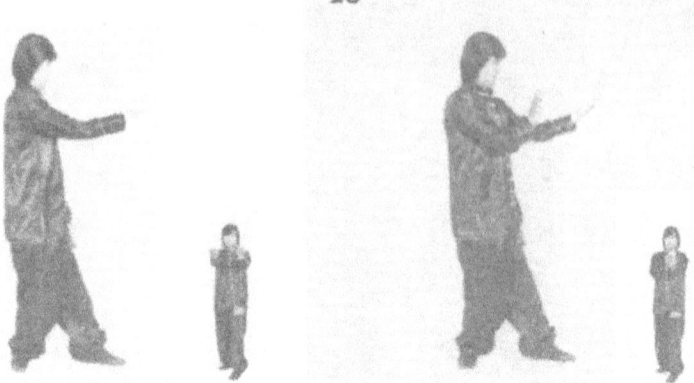

23 Shift back to left side and maintain position.

Side view of the previous position showing the hand position.

24 Extend both hands outward about shoulder-width with the palm still facing downward.

Keep the arms at shoulder level and do not go past the width of the body.

25 Turn both hands upward with the palm facing at a slight angle for double palm-up blocks.

The hands are turned inward. Notice the inward position as compared to the previous move.

26 Draw both hands into the centerline position keeping the left arm outward with palm up and the right hand facing with palm away from the body.

Both arms are in the centerline position protecting the body. The hands are in position with the right hand by the left elbow joint.

27 Now alternate the hands with the left hand turned inward with the palm facing outwardly and drawn back to the elbow. The right hand turned outward and extended forward.

Side view.

28 Switch hand and turn the right hand inward while drawing back and turn the left hand outward while extending it out.

Side view.

29 Turn the left hand with the palm turned inward toward the right side while withdrawing toward the elbow region of the right arm—a palm block. The right hand extended outward toward the center and strike out with a vertical palm strike.

Side view.

30 Now reverse the process with the right arm pulling back and left hand is thrust forward.

31
32

35
36

37
38

33    **34**

31 Alternate the left hand backward and strike with the right palm.

32 Withdraw the right arm into a tucked-back elbow block with the left hand drawn back to the arm pit area.

33 Turn the whole body toward the back with the elbow remaining in the same positioning.

34 Shift into a back leaning horse and drop the right arm into the blocking position with the left arm protecting the upper body.

35 Pull the right arm back to the side position and the left arm pulled back under the armpit,

36 Repeat the movement by blocking toward the front.

37 Pull back and repeat previous movement.

38 Maintaining the right arm in same position while placing the left arm into the centerline region and prepare to punch outwardly.

39

40

43

44

45

46

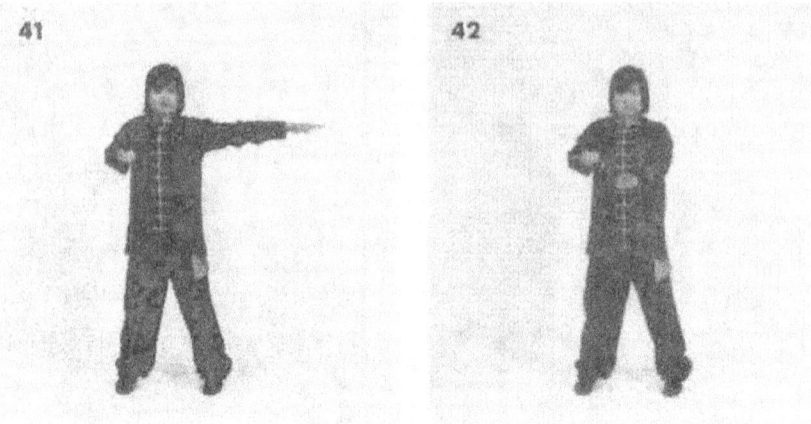

39 Extend the punch with the left arm while drawing the right arm back to the side position fist closed.

40 Pull the left punch back into an elbow block position, the forearm is parallel to the chest area and not drawn in.

41 Rotate the horse back to the front horse position and chop out to the left side with an open hand cut with the palm down.

42 Pull the hand down toward the stomach region with palm still down.

43 Slide your right hand down on top of the elbow region of the right arm with the hand open and palm up.

44 Slide the arm downward and out to an palm-up block while withdrawing the left hand back to starting position.

45 Now finishing off with the previously learned block, the hand is turned inward and down.

46 Close the hand in a grabbing motion.

47  **48**

51  **52**

53  **54**

49  **50**

47 Withdraw the hand completely while turning the fist back into the original starting position.

This finishes off the first section using the left-hand side. Now the movements are reversed and repeated on the right side. Numbers 48 to 76 are the opposite side of movements numbers 19 to 47.

48 Extend the two hands outward with the fingers in a horizontal position.
49 Withdraw the hand in toward your body with the left arm on top of the right arm and the palm facing down.
50 Shift the body to the right side keeping the arms in the same position.
51 Rotate to the left side.
52 Rotate back to the right side.
53 Extend both hands outward with a cutting motion.
54 Turn the hand upward with the arm bent.

55

56

59

60

63

64

55 Withdraw left hand back to right elbow region with both palms facing each other.
56 Reverse hand and pull the right hand back while the left hand turns up.
57 Repeat movement but with opposite hands.
58 Turn the right hand with the palm facing toward your left elbow while the left hand is thrust forward into a palm strike.
59 Turn the left palm in toward the right arm and strike with the right palm.
60 Repeat with the other side.
61 Withdraw the left arm back toward your body with the elbow up while the right arm is withdrawn to the underarm region.
62 Rotate the body to the left side while maintaining the same hand position.
63 Shift into a right side horse with the left hand making an inside block (bong sao) and right hand defending by the face.
64 Turn to the left side with the left arm up and right hand by your side.

65 Shift back to the right side and use an elbow up in the air block and right hand protecting the head area.
66 Turn back to left side with the left arm bent outward and right hand pulled back to side position.
67 Slide the right hand out toward the inside elbow region of your left arm.
68 Extend the punch outward following the centerline while the left hand pulls back to the side.
69 Withdraw the front half of your arm into an elbow-up block.
70 Pivot back to front horse and extend your right arm out to the side with palm down.
7 1 Circle the hand back in front of your body with a depressing palm block.
72 Draw your left hand on top of your right arm by the elbow joint.
73 Draw the right hand back to the side while extending the palm-up block to center of the body.
74 Turn the hand down toward the ground.

75

76

78

80

83

84

75   Close the fingers in a grabbing motion.
76   Withdraw the arm back to the side position.
77   Turn to the left side and extend the left arm up.
78   Take the front leg and raise it up to a front heel kick.
79   Step down and slide forward with the back leg dragging in toward the front. Use the right arm in a bong sau block.
80 Drop the right arm back down with the left hand on top to the side of the waist. Side view.
81 Extend kick outward with the heel. Side view of kick.
82 Drop the leg down and draw the back leg forward in a sliding motion using a side block.
83 Again drop the hand to the side as done previously.
84 Extend the kick.

85

86

89

90

93

94

85 Drop down and block with bong sau and move forward.
86 Drop the hand down to the side.
87 Extend the front leg into a heel kick.
88 Drop the leg and slide forward while sending the right hand into an uppercut, the left hand is withdrawn to the side.

*Note: in Wing Chun there are many repeated movements in a series whereas the technique is done three times over and then the same on the other side. This stresses the very important movements and also makes you capable of using either side.

89 Turn back to the front horse position and draw the punching arm back to a hand block shoulder level with palm downward.
90 Extend the hand out to the side.
91 Retract the hand and drop it in front of the body with a palm block.
92 Place your left hand across the elbow region of the right arm.
93 Pull the right arm back while sending the left hand out into a palm up block.
94 Rotate the hand downward, finger pointing down.

95

96

99

100

103

104

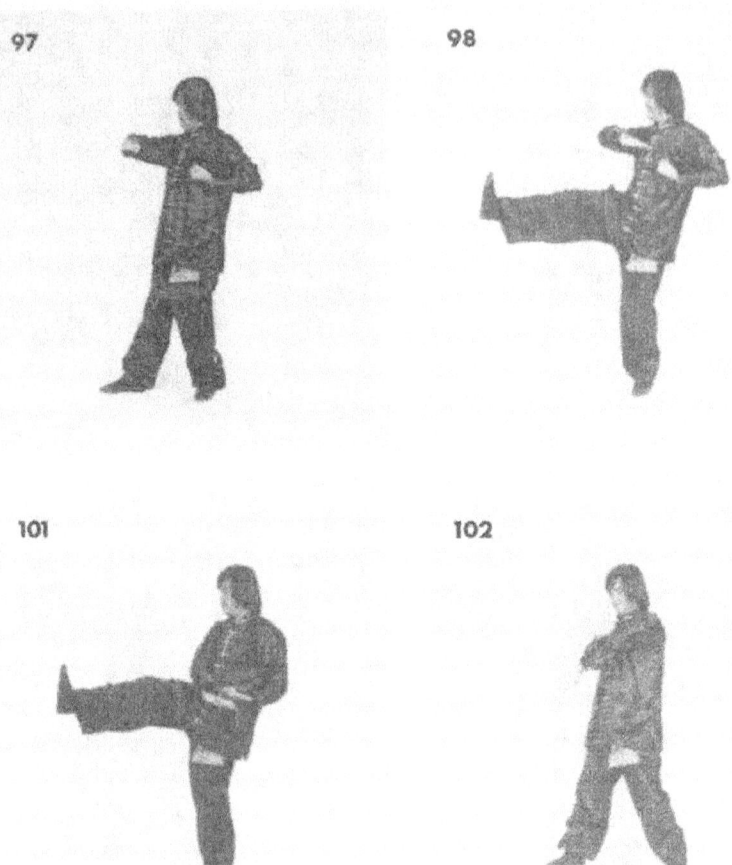

95 Close the hand in a grabbing motion.
96 Retract the hand back to the side.
97 Pivot the body to the right side with an arm level block with palm facing down.
98 Extend the kick to stomach level.
99 Drop the leg and slide forward with a bong sau block.
1 00 Drop the hand to the side with the hands crossing at the wrist.
2 01 Extend the kick with the heel.
1 02 Slide forward into a bong sau block drawing the back leg in toward the front. Make sure you are making some distance when performing this movement.
103 Drop the hand to the side.
1 04 Extend the kick.

105

106

109

110

113

114

- 1 05 Slide forward and block with the hand. 1 06 Drop the hand to the side.
- I 07 Extend a front heel kick.
- II 08 Slide forward and uppercut with the left hand and retract the right hand back to the side.

  *There are some teachers that stress more on the kick to maintain balance while others rely mainly on the hands. In some versions of Cham Kui the last three kicks in the previous sequences are not done but instead they follow through with the hand and eliminate the kick. Both ways are proper for practicing purposes. Yip Man did not teach it with the kicks but many of his top disciples have added it in just for training purposes to obtain better balance and coordination.

109 Pivot to front horse an elbow level block as shown.
- III 0 Extend the hand outward.
- I 1 1 Circle and drop in the center of the body palms down.
- II 2 Place right hand on the left elbow region.
- III 3 Slide forward and perform palm-up block. 114 Circle the hand downward.

115  **116**

119  **120**

123  **124**

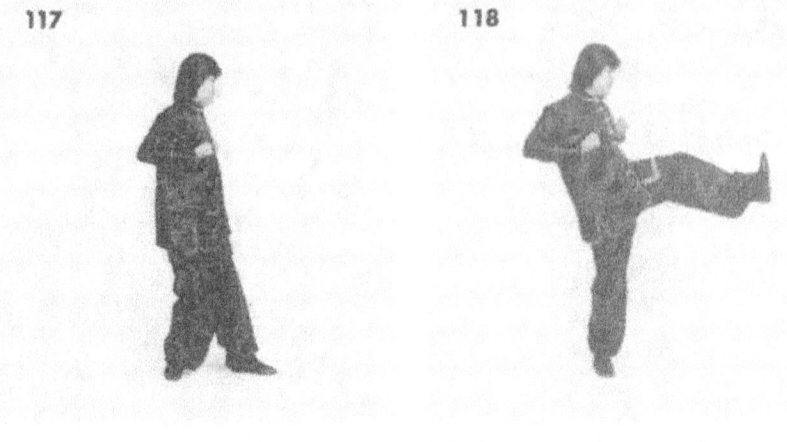

I   1 5 Use a grabbing motion while closing the fist.
II 1 6 Retract to starting position.
III 1 7 Pivot the body to the left side.
IV   8 Use a front heel kick.
11 9 Drop down and slide forward while using the two hands in a downward block. This is the essence of the form; it is known as Spanning the Gap or Spanning the Bridge move. This portion was to have bridged the span from kicking into the hand defense. The form got its name from this portion of the form. Side view of last movement.
120 Turn your hand upward with palm facing toward you. Side view.
1   21 Keeping the hand up, bring the leg up and kick forward.
122 Drop down and sliding forward while the hands are also lowered.
123 Invert the hand upward with palm facing upward.
1 24 Pull the leg up and kick forward.

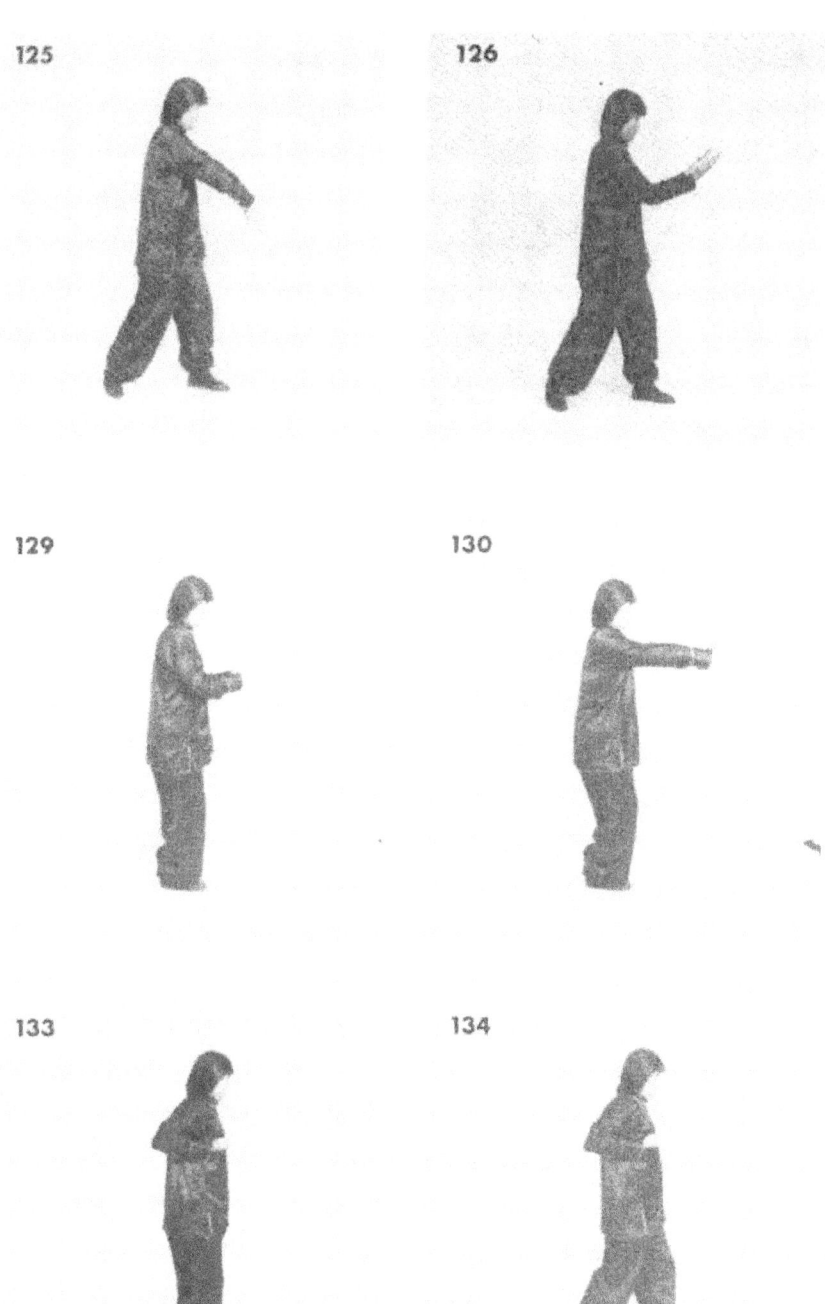

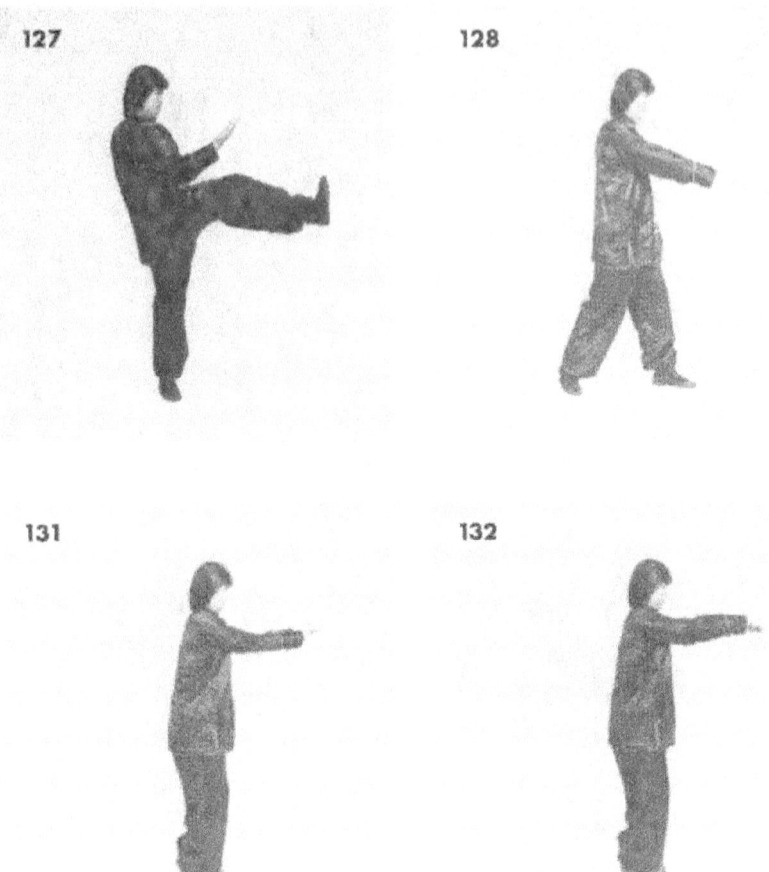

1 25 Drop the leg down and slide forward with the hand down blocking.
1 26 Turn the hand up.
1 27 Extend the kick.
1 28 Circle the hands outward and bring them together at waist level.
1 29 Bring your back leg forward toward the front with both legs together keeping the hand in the same position.
1 30 Extend the hand forward and pop the hands upward palm away from the body.
1 31 Turn the hand over with palm facing upward.
1 32 Rotate the hands and close the hand in a grabbing motion.
1 33 Redraw the hand to the armpit area.
2 34 Slide your right foot backward.

135

136

139

140

143

144

137 138

141 142

135   Pivot and turn your body completely toward the back.
1 36 Extend the front leg into a heel kick.
1 37 Drop the foot forward and slide the whole body forward while dropping the hand forward and down.

*The movements from 137 to 151 are the opposite side of the previous movements 11 8-134

1 38 Turn the hand up in a double outside palm • up block.
2 39 Kick with the front leg.
1 40 Slide forward and extend the hand going downward.
141   Turn the hand up.
142   Kick with the front leg.
143   Sliding forward and dropping the hand.
144   Invert the hand.

145  **146**

149  **150**

153  **154**

145 Kick with front heel kick.
146 Drop the leg and circle both hands outward, bring the hands back to gether in front of the body.
147 Draw the back leg up forward to the front leg.
148 Extend the hand forward and snap the wrist and fingers upward.
149 Turn the hands upward.
1 50 Rotate the hands and close them in a grabbing motion.
1 51 Retract the hand to the side of your body.
1 52 Turn the body toward the front at a 45-degree slant, feet together.
2 53 Raise the left leg up.
154 Kick forward with a front heel thrust.

155
156

159
160

163
164

157

158

161

162

1 55 Retract the leg to starting position.
1 56 Kick out toward the side with a side heel thrust making sure the toes are pulled back.
1 57 Drop the leg to the front.
1 58 Draw your right leg upward.
1 59 Kick directly in front of the body.
1 60 Retract the leg to starting position.
1 61 Kick out to the side.
1 62 Dirop the leg to the side: .

163 Pivot the body toward the right side and drop your left hand down in a palm block.
1 64 Pivot and block with right hand.

165

166

169

170

171

172

167   **168**

1 65 Rotate back to left-hand block.
2 66 Pivot back to the right-hand block.
3 67 Turn back to front horse position and punch with the left hand.
1 68 Punch with the right while drawing the left hand back.
1 69 Punch left hand while right hand pulls back.
1 70 Reverse the punching.
1 7 1 Withdraw the hand back to the side.
1 72 Draw your left leg in toward your right leg.

Finish of the second Wing Chun form, Cham Kui, or Searching for the Bridge. The form is also available on film through Sil Lum Supply Company.

Chapter VII

FREE SPARRING TECHNIQUES

Free sparring is the most advanced fighting level in many self-defense systems. Fighting at this level is depended more upon reflex action rather than prearranged fighting techniques. Complete knowledge of your system is thoroughly tested in this matter which utilizes both your mental and physical discipline.

There is no given situation, only spontaneous reaction to the immediate danger at hand. The importance of timing is essential in this phase of training coupled with the proper distancing of your opponent positioning. A block is insufficient if all it does is strike the air instead of your opponent punches or kicks. A wasted punch is just as bad if all it does is punch the air while not only wasting energy but also leaving yourself open for a counterattack by a more experienced fighter.

The only way to practice free fighting is with a live opponent which is capable of launching, punching and kicking back at you. A person may have a tremendous amount of speed and techniques while fighting the air but with a live opponent it is a totally different concept. Now the opponent can really hurt you if you are not completely familiar with your own fighting skills. Do not rely on letter-perfect techniques that you may have learned in prearranged fighting pattern. In a real fighting situation a person is never going to throw the same type of punch as they would in the street or even from various systems. Learn to adapt to the situation and maneuver your body to give yourself the best advantage possible.

Never get stale by just fighting your own classmate and your own style. Many of your techniques may be useless against various techniques from other systems if used in only one particular way. A modification of your technique may be necessary to be readjusted to coup with the situation. This is by no means for you to go and challenge students from different systems. One can learn to work with other styles and exchange ideals and techniques. Get permission from your teacher and also the permission of the other person instructor also. This will show signs of respect and is in no way a threat to his system of teaching.

Learn from one another and don't put down another man's style just because his is different from yours. Following are just a few techniques on free sparring. Again this is done in a pattern to explain some of the techniques in the Wing Chun system.

1. Ready position.
2. The attacker on the right throws a left punch which is met with a right rising wrist block that sends the punch upward into the air.
3. The defender on the left pivots his body toward the left and rotates the wrist strike into a knife-edge strike to the side of the face.
4. But before the strike can reach its destination the attacker uses an inside palm block to deflect the blow.
5. The defender then pivots in toward the attacker and applies an elbow wrist lock to the opponent's right arm. Any type of follow-up from this position will render your opponent inoperable.

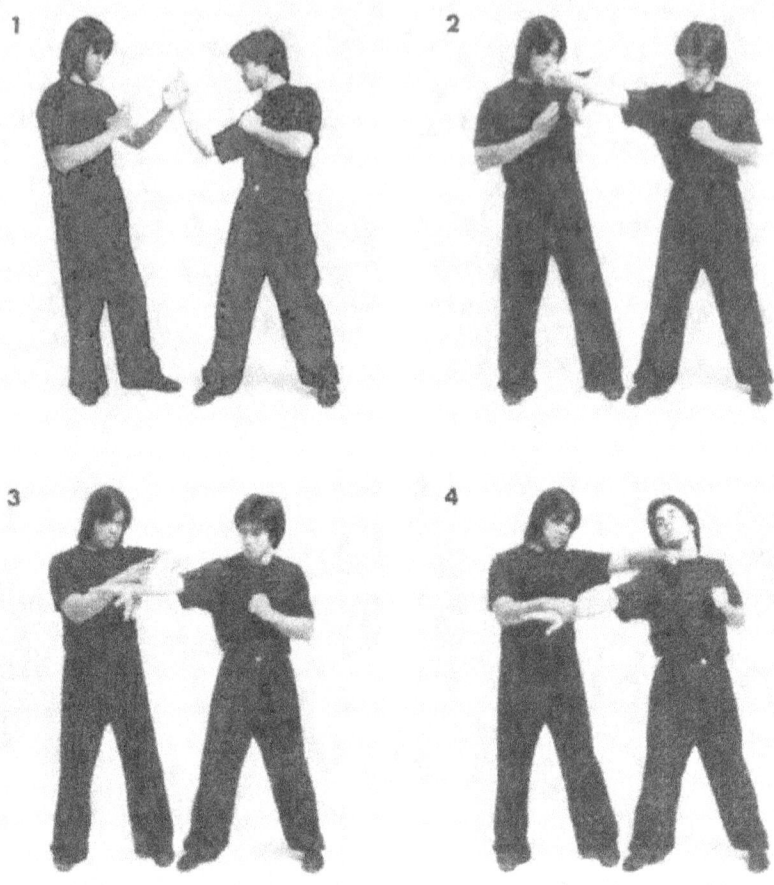

1 Ready position.
2 Opponent throws a right punch which is met with a left bong sau or elbow in the air block—pivot the body at the same time.
3 Use your right hand to come on top of your opponents striking arm.
4 Grab the hand and pull the opponent in toward you while releasing the blocking hand into an open hand strike to the throat area.

1. Fighting position.
2. Your opponent throws a left punch which is met with an outside wrist block with the pivoting of the body. The pivot adds power to your block.
3. Now rotate the body back toward your opponent and strike to the collarbone area while grabbing hold of his right hand with your left.
4. After the strike convert the striking hand into a neck grab while drawing the rear leg in toward your opponent. This motion gives you more power to pull your opponent off balance while also preventing him from launching his own offense attacks.
5. Bring the knee upward and draw the opponent's head downward at the same time causing a very dangerous but powerful offensive movement.
6. Pivot the body and apply a heel thrust to the opponents knee region while still maintaining control of his upper body.

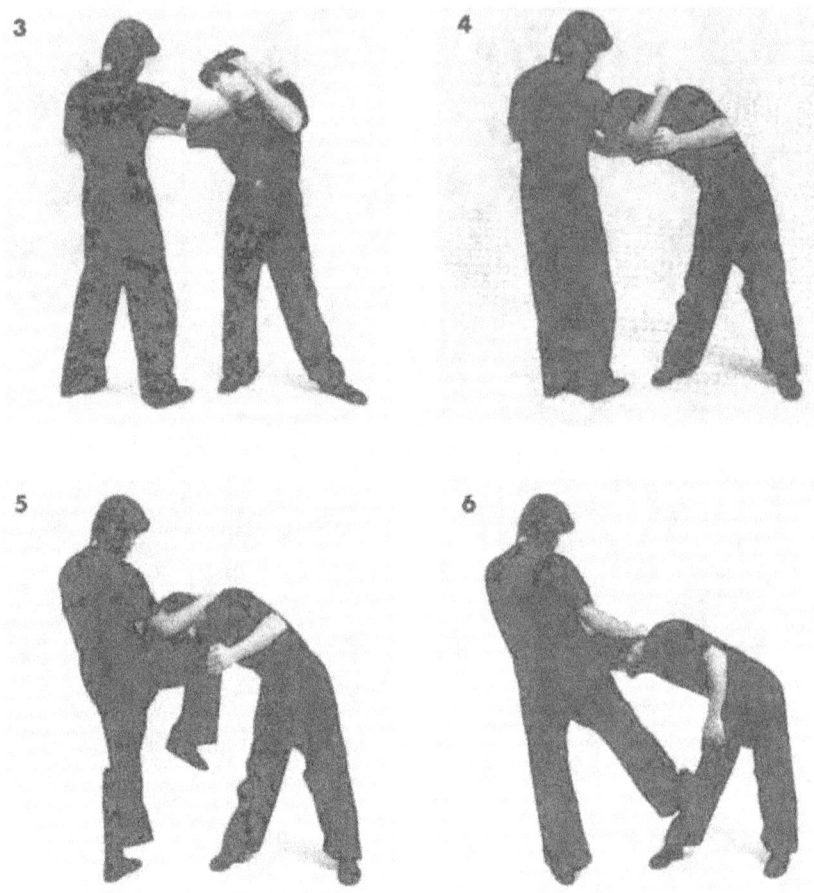

1 Ready position both opponents with their left side out.

2 Opponent draws his right leg up to attempt a roundhouse kick.

3 Defender waits until the leg is almost extended and then drops his front hand into a side block which hits the opponent in the shin area. Make sure you are pivoting at the same time you apply the block.

4 Sliding inward toward your opponent throw a low wrist strike into the groin area while the other hand controls your opponent's hand.

1 Ready position, the attacker is in a tiger ready position.
2 The opponent strikes out with a double Tiger Strike which is met with an inside high block and an outside low block.
3 The top hand is dropped on top of the opponents hand—a depressing palm block which forces the hands together. The left hand is set for punching.
4 Defender sends a left cross punch into the opponent's face while still pressing the hand down and away.

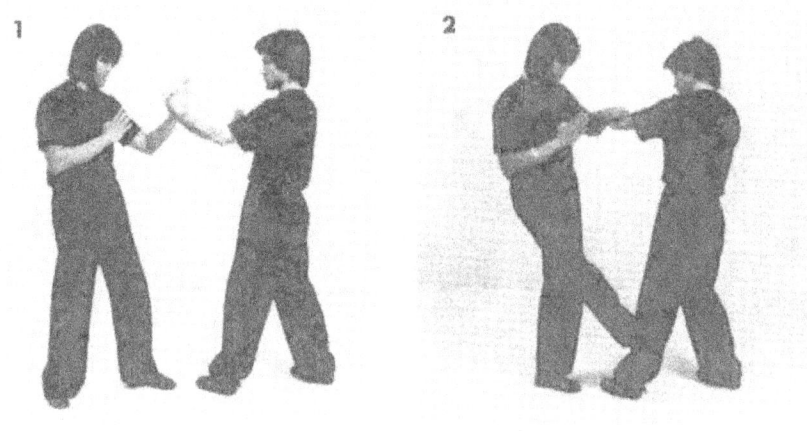

1. Ready position.
2. Grab opponent's hand and apply a cross heel kick to the shin area.
3. Turn the foot and step down while applying a punch to the jaw.

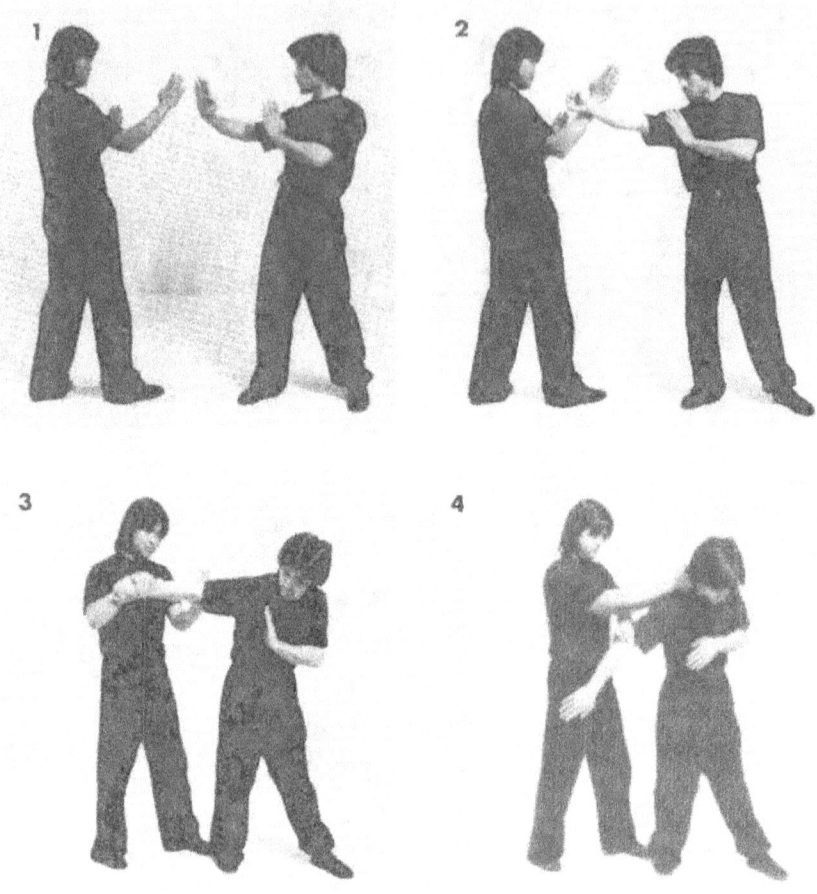

1. Ready position.
2. The opponent throws a right punch which is met with an outside palm block.
3. Stepping into the opponent rotate the blocking hand into a wrist grab and use the left hand to push against the elbow joint. This applies pressure to the opponent's body which turns him downward.
4. Push his arm down with your left hand and punch to the back of the ear area with a straight punch.

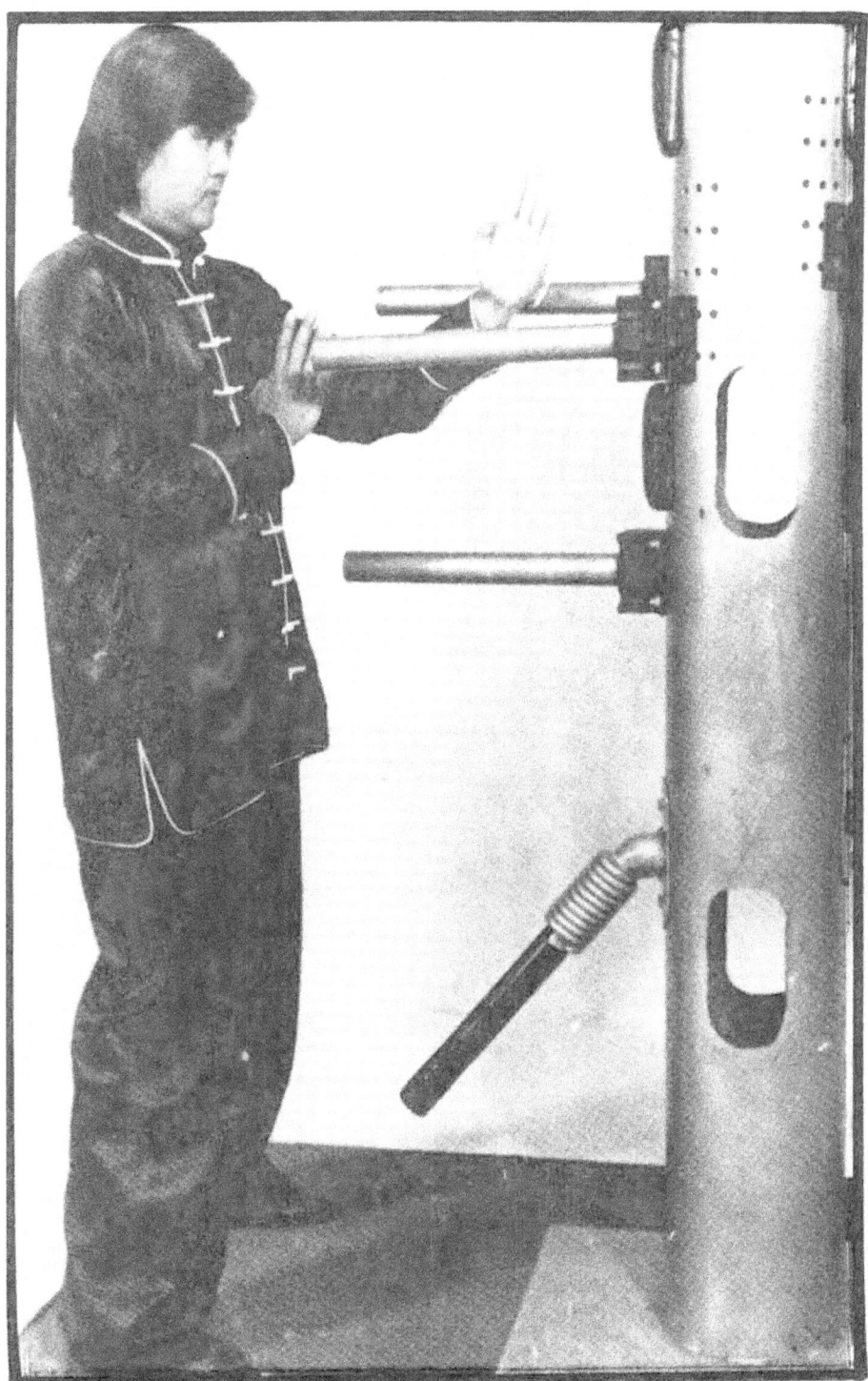

Chapter IX

WING CHUN OTHER ASPECTS
WEAPONS AND DUMMY TRAINING

The Wing Chun system is a simple but complete system which contains hand forms, weaponry, medical application, and fighting techniques. Based on the philosophy of simplicity and economy of motion which characterize this unique system the fighting techniques are very simple but effective. The Wing Chun system consists of three hand sets which have been mentioned before. They are: Sil Lum Tao (Small Idea); Cham Kui (Searching the Bridge); and Bil Jee (Flying Fingers).

The two weapon set consists of the Butterfly Knife and the Long Pole techniques. The pole or staff is a nine-foot wooden object which is known today as the Six and ⅝ Point Pole Form which was taught originally in the Hung Gar system. But many of the techniques have been changed to fit the Wing Chun system of practice. The other weapon is the short butterfly knife called Bat Joh Do which can use the many hand techniques learned in Wing Chun.

The wooden dummy technique is another famous training equipment used in this system but many other systems also use some type of dummy training as well. The 108 dummies used in the Shaolin Temple are probably the most famous and the most widely imitated.

In the future a second book will cover the more advanced techniques which will cover the Wooden Dummy techniques, Bil Jee the 3rd Wing Chun form, and also Chi Gerk or Sticky Leg techniques.

Position of using butterfly knives.

Wing Chun 6% Point Long Pole Technique

1 Starting position of Wing Chun Dummy Training.

2-6 The following are just some of the basic movements used on the dummy.

Palm-up block with punch on the dummy.

Palm-up block.

Inside block using bong sao.

Bong sao.

Double block.

Straight punch and hook.

Conclusion

If there is something to be said for practicality, there is something to be said for Wing Chun Kung-Fu. Indeed, the arts conservation of movement theory and, as this book's author puts it, the "no-nonsense approach" to achieving a goal, may well prove to be more adaptable to our contemporary culture than any other single style of Kung-Fu emanating from pre-Communist China.

Wing Chun is what you might call an "anti-complication" system concerned with stripping away the flower and show found in many other systems. It strives to cut through the array of techniques, complexities and dubious theories which seem inherent to many Kung-Fu forms, using straightforward punching. Wing Chun reflects, in its techniques, an attitude which one of my previous teachers exhibited when asked which technique was proper for overcoming a specific attack. He replied, "To hell with all that, just hit the guy in the nose."

Of course being able to just "hit the guy in the nose" would be nice, I guess. The problem is—how? Wing Chun offers an answer. Perhaps one of the best answers available.

In this text Douglas Wong introduces (among other things) the second Wing Chun form, for the first time in the English language. This form, called *Searching for the Bridge*, has something to offer nearly every style of martial art as every system is basically caught up in the problem involved with bridge-work. Mr. Wong is also working on supplementary volumes explaining the detailed use of the Mook-Yan-Jeong (Wooden Dummy) and Blindfolded-fighting techniques.

Michael P. Staples

www.ingramcontent.com/pod-product-compliance
Lightning Source LLC
Chambersburg PA
CBHW070946230426
43666CB00011B/2580